BUILDING
OUTDOOR FURNITURE

Classic Deck, Patio & Garden Projects
That Will Last a Lifetime

Edited by
CHAD McCLUNG

Contents

The Haycock Adirondack

A modern tweak to a classic design marries comfort and style.

By Paul Anthony and Ken Burton

The Adirondack chair is synonymous with the best of summer: You know, relaxing in the shade with friends and family, or simply sittin' back on a warm evening with a drink in hand. These iconic chairs, with rear legs that lean forward to become part of the seat structure, come in many forms, and are made of everything from construction lumber to injection-molded plastic. But some Adirondack chairs aren't that comfortable. Others are so deep and low that they're hard to get out of. Many are huge, heavy, and difficult to move.

That's why we took notice of this design by Haycock Township, PA-based architect and furniture maker Ric Hanisch. Its curved and tapered geometry combines ergonomics and style to create a chair that invites relaxation but that sits high enough to easily rise from. It's comfortable, compact, and portable enough to move around easily. The comfort lies partially in the outwardly tapered configuration of the seat and arms. The seat's shape mimics the natural splay of relaxed legs, while the arms keep elbows comfortably close to the body. Also, the back splats angle rearward to create a slight curvature for your back, and include a release gap for your spine. The overall effect is that of your body nestling into the chair. Nice.

Having few square corners, this project involves a fair amount of cut-to-fit work, which makes the build enjoyably challenging. You'll see. We built ours from thermally modified poplar for durability and light weight. Other good outdoor woods include cedar, cypress, and mahogany.

A solid structure with simple connections

The base of the chair consists of two sides **(F)** connected by slats **(B)** screwed to their upper edges. A temporary brace holds the sides in place for the slat attachment. Each leg consists of a tapered front **(J)** and side **(I)** piece screwed together and fastened to a spacer **(H)**attached to its base side. The twin back splat assembly attaches to the base via a back support slat and back blocks **(G)** attached to the sides. The arms **(D)** connect the legs to the back via the arm support **(C)** to tie everything together.

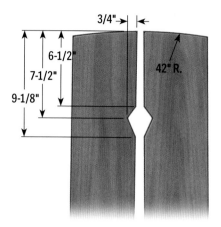

Figure 1: Back Cutout Detail

3/4"
6-1/2"
7-1/2"
9-1/8"
42" R.

Figure 2: Arm and Side Pattern

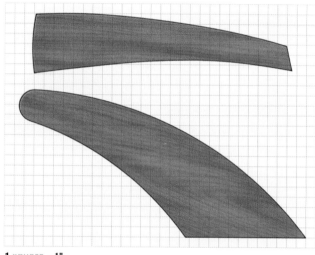

1 square = 1"

Figure 3: Side Layout Template

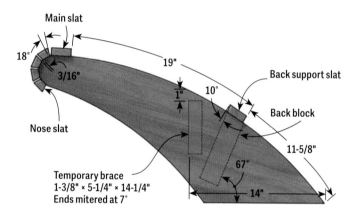

Main slat
18°
3/16"
Nose slat
19"
1"
10°
Back support slat
Back block
11-5/8"
Temporary brace
1-3/8" × 5-1/4" × 14-1/4"
Ends mitered at 7°
67°
14"

Figure 4: Elevations

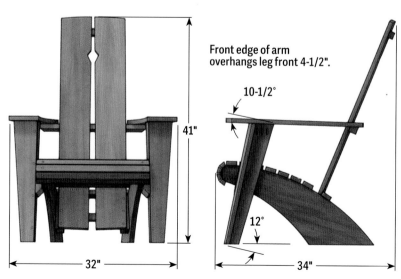

Front edge of arm overhangs leg front 4-1/2".
10-1/2°
41"
32"
12°
34"

Order of Work

1. Build base.
2. Make and attach slats.
3. Make legs.
4. Make back.
5. Attach back.

Make the shoulder cuts. Use a backsaw to cut the notch shoulders, guiding off the layout lines on both faces of the workpiece.

Flatten the notch bottoms. Use a chisel to even up the bottoms of the notches, ensuring that depths equal one-half of the part widths.

Build the cross frames

NOTE: Before building, take a minute to inspect your stock and select the best boards. Any chips, knots, or bad spots should be kept on the underside faces or cut out when laying out parts. Any crowned faces should face up once fastened in place to better shed water. The most visible parts, or those that will be in contact with arms and legs, must be smooth and splinter free.

1. Now, working with either dimensional lumber or thicker stock that you joint and plane to the part thicknesses in the **Cut List**, crosscut the left and right seat frame parts **(A)** and left and right tabletop frame parts **(B)** to length. Also, cut the eight spacers **(C)** to size **(Figure 1)**.

2. Lay out the centered notches on both faces of the seat frame parts **(A)** and tabletop frame parts **(B)**, (notch detail, **Figure 1**). Here, measure

the thickness of the combined frame parts and spacer **(C)** when sandwiched together for the notch widths. The mating notches must fit snugly. Make the shoulder cuts **(Photo A)**. Then make multiple cuts between the shoulder cuts to the baseline of the notch. Cut out the waste with a chisel and mallet. Repeat for the other notches.

3. At the miter saw, bevel-cut the ends of the left and right seat frame parts **(A)** and left and right tabletop frame parts **(B)** at 67-1/2° (see **Figure 1** for the bevel orientations).

4. Working on a flat surface such as a workbench, group the left and right seat frame parts **(A)** and the left and right table frame parts **(B)**, orienting each group with their notches up.

Install the spacers. Tap the spacers against the intersecting seat and table frame parts. Make them flush along the edges of the frame pairs.

Draw a reference line. With the bottom ends of the parts aligned against a backstop, strike a reference line along the top end of the seat leg and across the face of the table leg.

Construct the seats. Align a seat leg to a seat base on a benchtop as shown, clamping the assembly to the bench. Then drill counterbored holes and drive the screws.

Align the part ends and clamp them together and to the workbench. Clean up the notches **(Photo B)**.

TIP: I cut a screw hole–marking jig out of thin plywood to the same length and width as the spacers (C) (Photo C). I drilled two 1/16" holes in the jig indicating screw locations. Using it, I marked consistent screw hole locations with an awl. I flipped the jig when marking holes on the opposite side of the cross-frame assemblies so opposing screws didn't contact each other.

5. On a level surface, test-assemble the interlocking seat **(A)** and table **(B)** cross frames, fitting in spacers **(C)** (notch detail in **Figure 1**, **Photo C**). Disassemble.

6. Use exterior glue in all of the joints. Reassemble the frame parts. Mark the screw hole locations, and drill counterbored pilot holes.

Starting at the mating notch joints, drive four exterior-grade 3" screws vertically to join the seat and table frame pieces **(A, B)**. Drive 3" screws through the frame sides and into spacers **(C)**. Repeat for all spacer joints.

Cut the parts & assemble the seat bases

1. Using 1-1/2"-thick × 5-1/2"-wide stock, cut the table legs **(D)**, seat bases **(E)**, and seat legs **(F)** to length and to correct angles **(Figure 2)**.

2. Place a seat leg **(F)** on a table leg **(D)**, aligning the bottom ends using a backstop **(Photo D)**. Strike a

Apply glue, and set the base assembly on the table leg. Center and align the leg on the seat base between matching spacers. Drill the holes and drive the screws.

G

Apply glue to the seat frames. Set aside the base assembly with its alignment stops while spreading glue on the hard-to-get-at mating surfaces of the seat frames.

H

Check the alignment. Place a straightedge across the top ends of the seat legs and top edges of the seat frames to make sure the mating assemblies are aligned.

reference line on the table leg. This will come into play in Step 4 and again when attaching the seat cross frame later. Similarly, strike lines on the remaining legs. Continue the lines across the edges and opposite faces of the table legs.

3. Fasten a seat base **(E)** to two seat legs **(F)** using three 3" screws per leg driven into counterbored holes **(Photo E)**. Note that the seat legs should be flush with the ends

of the seat bases **(Figure 1)**. Repeat for all four seat base assemblies.

4. Make a pair of angled seat base spacers **(Figure 2)**. Next, clamp a table leg **(D)** in your bench vise with the top end down, aligning the reference lines with the surface of your benchtop. Now, using the spacers, fasten a seat base/seat leg assembly **(E/F)** to the bottom end of the leg with 3" screws and exterior glue **(Photo F)**. Mark and

counterbore three centered holes in the joining parts and drive the screws. Repeat to make the remaining three base assemblies **(D/E/F)**.

5. Cut eight seat cleats **(G)** to size, and glue and screw them with 2-1/2" screws to the inside faces of the seat legs **(F)**. Extend them 7/8" beyond the outside edges of the legs, and make their top edges flush with the leg top ends.

Add the base assemblies to the seat cross frames

1. Strike lines 13-3/4" in from the ends across the top edges of the seat cross frames assembly **(A/C)**. This line tells where the table legs **(D)** intersect the top edges of the seat frame assembly.

2. Clamp a pair of scrap alignment stops along the top of the reference lines on the sides of a table leg **(D)**. Dry-fit the leg of the base assembly

Figure 3: Biscuit Slot Marking Jig

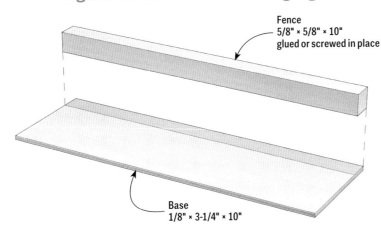

Fence
5/8" × 5/8" × 10"
glued or screwed in place

Base
1/8" × 3-1/4" × 10"

Mark the biscuit positions. Hold the biscuit marking jig fence along the outside edge of the perimeter boards to mark consistent biscuit slot centers with a pencil.

Cut the biscuit slots. While firmly holding a perimeter board in place, align the biscuit joiner centerline with the mark, and plunge-cut the slot.

(E/F/G) in place between the seat frames **(A)**, aligning the reference lines and resting the stops on the top edges of the frames. Next, mark the screw locations on the outside face of one seat frame. (As before, I made and used a plywood marking jig for this.) Slide the base assembly out of the way, and apply glue in the base assembly/ seat frames mating area **(Photo G)**.

3. Slide the base assembly **(D/E/F/G)** into place **(Photo H)**. Once all the key parts align, drill counterbored holes for 3" screws. Repeat the process for attaching the remaining base assemblies to the seat frame cross assembly **(A/C)**.

Form the tabletop perimeter frames

1. Set up your miter saw to 22-1/2° (once cut, the miter angle of the board will be 67-1/2°). Verify the angle with a test cut. Using a stop to establish consistent lengths, angle-cut the top perimeter boards **(H)** and the bottom perimeter boards **(I)** to length **(Figure 2)**.

2. Using a square, or with a shop-made marking jig, mark the biscuit locations on the ends of the perimeter boards **(H, I) (Figure 3, Photo I)**.

NOTE: All top perimeter boards receive biscuit slots; only the mating ends of the bottom perimeter board pairs receive slots.

3. Adhere a 3/8"-thick spacer to your biscuit jointer with double-faced tape, and cut biscuit slots that are centered on the thickness

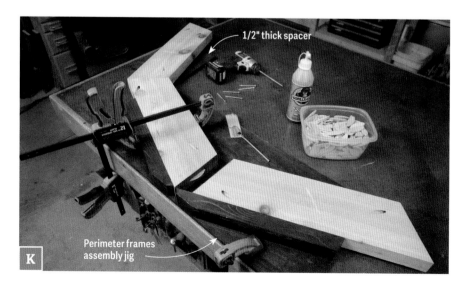

Assemble the top perimeter. With the assembly jig clamped to the table and one perimeter piece clamped to its fence, glue and screw the top perimeter boards end to end.

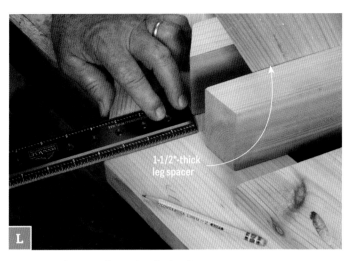

Measure the margins. Check the distance from the octagon's corners to the ends of the tabletop cross frames to center the latter. You want the same length all around.

Assemble the bottom perimeter. Working a quadrant at a time, glue and screw the chevron-like bottom board sections to the top cross frame assembly and octagon.

of the top and bottom perimeter boards **(H, I)**. Align the centerline of the tool with the marks made in Step 2. Cut the slots **(Photo J)**.

4. Build the perimeter frames assembly jig using scrap plywood and solid stock **(Figure 4)**.

5. Drill pocket holes on the bottom faces of the top perimeter boards **(H)** at the ends to fortify the biscuit joints and to snug up the pieces during assembly. Position the holes at least 3/4" in from the edges. Be sure the hole locations do not cause the screws to exit the edges of the perimeter boards. Now, working on a large, flat surface, apply glue in the

slots, insert the biscuits, and place two top perimeter pieces bottom faces up in the assembly jig. Drive the pocket screws to snug the joint. Move the assembly and fasten another perimeter board **(Photo K)**. Fit a spacer under the cantilevered end of the assembly to keep it level. Add a fourth board to make one-half of the octagonal top perimeter frame. Build the other half. Let the glue set up.

TIP: Apply a few strips of clear packing tape or coat of wax to the jig to keep the parts from sticking.

6. Drill two pocket holes on the bottom faces of the non-mating ends of the bottom perimeter boards making up the four chevron-like frame sets. Use the assembly jig to glue up the sets. Set the four frame sets aside to let the glue cure.

Figure 4: Perimeter Frames Assembly Jig

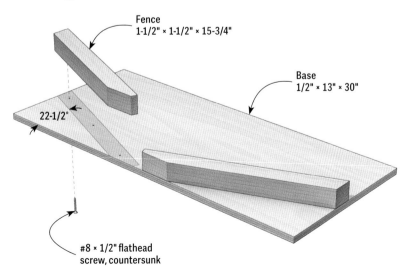

Fence
1-1/2" × 1-1/2" × 15-3/4"

Base
1/2" × 13" × 30"

22-1/2°

#8 × 1/2" flathead
screw, countersunk

Attach the legs to the tabletop. Drill counterbored pilot holes through the table frames and into the table legs. Drive screws to firmly fasten the legs in place.

7. Next, glue and screw the two half frames together to make the octagonal top perimeter frame. (I used a strap clamp to help tighten one half frame against the other.) After the glue sets up, remove the strap.

Attach the tabletop cross frame assembly

1. With the octagonal perimeter frame **(H)** top face down on a large assembly surface, place the tabletop cross frame assembly **(B/C)** on the octagon's bottom face. Insert and clamp scrap 1-1/2"-thick leg spacers between the tabletop frame parts to fix their overall dimension for installing the chevron-like bottom perimeter board sections **(I)**. Center the tabletop cross frame assembly on the octagonal frame **(Photo L)**. Mark the locations.

2 Now, using pocket screws and glue, secure the chevron-like bottom perimeter board **(I)** sections to the tabletop cross frame assembly

(B/C) (Photo M). Use 2-1/2" screws in counterbored holes to fasten the board sections to the octagonal frame **(H)**. Remove the leg spacers.

Cut & install the tabletop boards

1. Solicit a helper to flip the tabletop and top cross frame assembly right side up. Now, measure and cut to length the tabletop boards **(J, K)** listed in the **Cut List (Figure 2)**. For the best results, measure, cut, and fit the outside tabletop boards **(J)** flush against the octagonal perimeter frame **(H)**. Lay the outside tabletop boards in place.

2. Next, measure the distance between the outside tabletop boards **(J)**. Subtract from that measurement the combined widths of the remaining tabletop boards **(K, L)**. Divide the remaining number by six to determine the spacing between the tabletop

boards. Plane or resaw several spacers at that thickness. (My spacers measured 3/8" thick.)

3. Angle-cut one end of the outside adjacent tabletop boards **(K)**, leaving the other ends long. Fit the spacers between the outside tabletop boards **(J)** and the outside adjacent tabletop boards **(K)**. Mark the square ends of the boards for a good fit and angle-cut them. Lay them in place.

4. Cut three center tabletop boards **(L)** to fit. Angle-cut the corners of outside center tabletop boards as needed to maintain the spacing.

5. Using the spacers, fit the tabletop boards in place, and drill counterbored holes in the ends (two holes per end). Apply glue, and drive 2-1/2" screws to fasten them to the chevron-like bottom perimeter board sections **(I)**.

Octagonal Picnic Table Supply & Cut List

	Part	Thickness	Width	Length	Qty.
A	Left and right seat frame	1-1/2"	3-1/2"	88-3/16"	4
B	Left and right table frame	1-1/2"	3-1/2"	48"	4
C	Frame spacer	1-1/2"	3-1/2"	3-1/2"	8
D	Table leg	1-1/2"	5-1/2"	33-1/8"	4
E	Seat base	1-1/2"	5-1/2"	24"	4
F	Seat leg	1-1/2"	5-1/2"	14"	8
G	Seat cleat	1-1/2"	1-1/2"	9"	8
H	Top perimeter board	1-1/2"	5-1/2"	21-5/16"	8
I	Bottom perimeter board	1-1/2"	5-1/2"	16-1/8"	8
J*	Outside tabletop board	1-1/2"	5-1/2"	28-1/2"	2
K*	Outside adjacent tabletop board	1-1/2"	5-1/2"	39-15/16"	2
L	Center tabletop board	1-1/2"	5-1/2"	40-1/2"	3
M	Outside left and right seat board	1-1/2"	5-1/2"	26"	8
N	Inside left and right seat	1-1/2"	5-1/2"	23-5/8"	8
	Supplies				
	#8 exterior-grade screws			2-1/2"	
	#8 exterior-grade screws			3"	

Indicates parts that are initially cut oversized. See instructions.

Add the base & seats

1. With helpers, flip the tabletop and attached cross frame assembly upside down. Mark the center of the tabletop cross frame opening on the bottom face of the center tabletop board **(L)**. Drill a small pilot hole through the board. Next, saw a 1-1/2" × 1-1/2" × 36" piece of scrap.

2. Apply glue on the inside faces of the ends of the table frames **(B/C)**. Carefully lift the base assembly, turn it upside down, and fit the table legs **(D)** between the members of the table frames **(B)**. Insert the 1-1/2"-square piece into the center openings of the frames to align the seat frames over the table frames. Remove the 1-1/2" piece. Now, counterbore holes, and drive 3" screws to secure the base to the tabletop **(Photo N)**.

3. With helpers, flip the entire octagonal picnic table right side up and set it on a flat surface. Using a 1-1/2" Forstner bit, bore the umbrella hole, guiding on the pilot hole drilled in Step 1. Lay out the seat parts **(M, N)** to the sizes in the **Cut List** and appropriate angles **(Figure 2)**. Cut the pieces. Finally, using the same spacing for the tabletop boards, fasten the seat parts to the seat legs and cleats **(F, G)**, using glue and 2-1/2" screws in counterbored holes.

4. Cut plugs from cedar scrap. Then, glue the plugs in place to cover up the hardware. Flush-cut the plugs, and plane or sand them even.

5. Sand the octagonal picnic table to 180 grit. Using a 1/4"-radius roundover bit in a handheld router, round over the umbrella opening and all exposed seat and table edges. Wipe the surfaces clean and finish. I sprayed on Sikkens Cetol SRD.

Adirondack Glider

Rock the day away in your favorite outdoor spot with this American classic.

By Robert J. Settich

There's a reason the Adirondack chair is the most popular spot to relax in the great outdoors. Its angled back and wide armrests are designed to take the load off your feet while your body relaxes into the calm of summer. The only problem with an Adirondack chair is that you're chilling solo and not snuggled next to your loved one. With this expanded take on the American classic, you can now glide through a summer evening with a companion by your side.

Because I used poplar, which is prone to rot outdoors, I protected the wood with two coats of primer and two coats of exterior paint. For a clear wood look, go with rot-resistant cedar, cypress, or other exterior wood, and apply a clear UV (ultraviolet) resistant finish. Go with exterior screws and glue to guarantee long-lasting joints. Use the patterns to help you make the shaped parts.

Figure 1: Exploded View

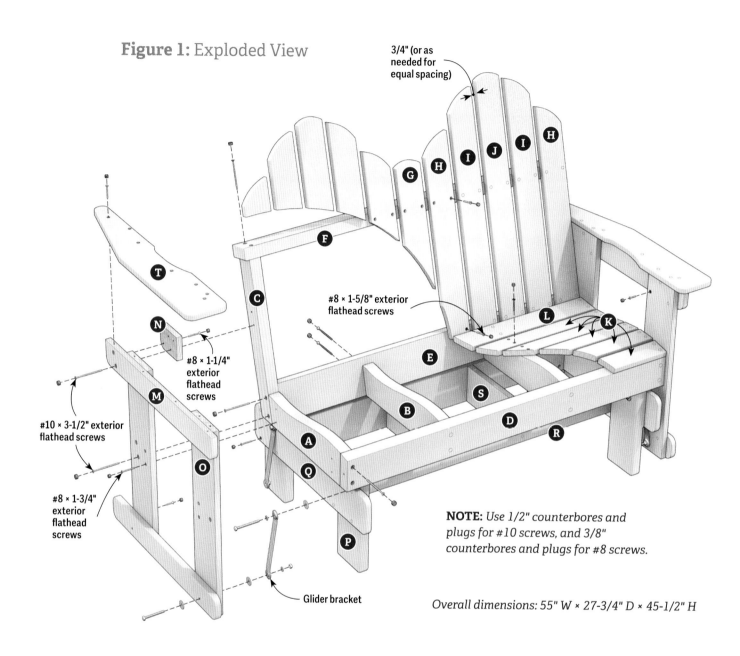

3/4" (or as needed for equal spacing)

#8 × 1-5/8" exterior flathead screws

#8 × 1-1/4" exterior flathead screws

#10 × 3-1/2" exterior flathead screws

#8 × 1-3/4" exterior flathead screws

Glider bracket

NOTE: *Use 1/2" counterbores and plugs for #10 screws, and 3/8" counterbores and plugs for #8 screws.*

Overall dimensions: 55" W × 27-3/4" D × 45-1/2" H

Cut the seat frame parts

NOTE: *Each of the seat end assemblies (A/C) are cut identically, allowing for fewer setups at the table saw. In this case, they are not mirror images.*

1. Crosscut 20"-long blanks from 1-1/2"-thick dressed stock for the end seat rails **(A)** and middle

seat rails **(B) (Figures 1 and 2)**. Cut 1-1/2"-thick blanks to 21" long for the back supports **(C)**.

2. Enlarge and transfer the seat rail pattern **(Figure 9)** to one of the blanks for the seat rails **(A, B)**. Bandsaw to the waste side of the line. Then sand the curves of one blank to the line,

using a disc sander for the convex curves and an oscillating spindle sander for the concave curves, taking care to keep the edges square. You cut the waste at the back end later.

3. Using this first rail **(A)** as a template, trace the curve onto the remaining blanks. Bandsaw

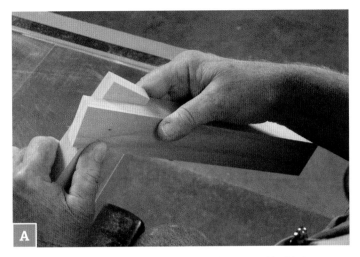

Cut some test pieces. Test-cut scrap pieces and hold them together to confirm the rabbet depths and angle settings.

Cut the half-laps. With the miter gauge fence angled at 15°, cut the half-lap joints with a dado set, starting at the shoulder cutline. A stopblock ensures consistent results.

the blanks, again cutting to the waste side of the line.

4. Adhere the completed rail **(A)** to one of the remaining bandsawn blanks with double-faced tape, aligning the bottom edges and front ends. Chuck a flush-trim bit into your table-mounted router, and smooth the bandsawn edge, guiding off the template. Flush-trim the other blanks to create identical curved edges.

5. Install a 3/4" dado set into your table saw and set it for a 3/4"-deep cut to make the half-lap joints for the end seat rails **(A)** and the back supports **(C)**. (See the seat rail assembly in **Figure 2**.) Attach an extension to your miter gauge and angle the gauge for a 15° half-lap cut. Confirm the height and angle settings with test cuts in two pieces of scrap lumber that match the thickness of the wood for parts A and C **(Photo A)**.

6. Once your test pieces fit nicely, cut a 2-1/2" rabbet 3/4" deep in the end seat rails **(A) (Photo B)**. Cut a 3-5/8" rabbet 3/4" deep into the back supports **(C)**. After making the initial shoulder cuts, remove the stopblock to cut away the remainder of the waste of each part. If necessary, clean up the sawn surfaces with a sanding block or rabbet plane.

7. Using an exterior-grade adhesive, glue and clamp each end seat rail **(A)** to its back support **(C)**. Let the glue dry overnight.

8. Flush-cut the waste at the angled joint ends of parts A and C with a handsaw.

9. Crosscut the top ends of the back supports **(C)** to their final lengths at the table saw or miter saw.

Seat frame assembly

1. Referring to the **Cut List**, rip a 10° bevel on one edge of a 46"-long piece of 1-1/2" stock for the seat front **(D)** **(Figure 2)**. Now rip the part to final width, matching the width of the front ends of the end seat rails **(A)**.

2. Drill the counterbores and clearance holes in the seat front **(D) (Figure 2)**.

3. Chuck a 1/8" roundover bit into your table-mounted router, and rout the bottom front edge of the seat front rail **(D)**. Leave the router set up, as you'll need it several more times for other glider parts.

4. Clamp the seat front rail **(D)** to the two seat end assemblies **(A/C)**. I cut a pair of scrapwood cauls at 15° for use at the angled back end of the assembly to prevent the bar clamps from slipping. Check for square, and

Figure 2: Glider Seat Frame

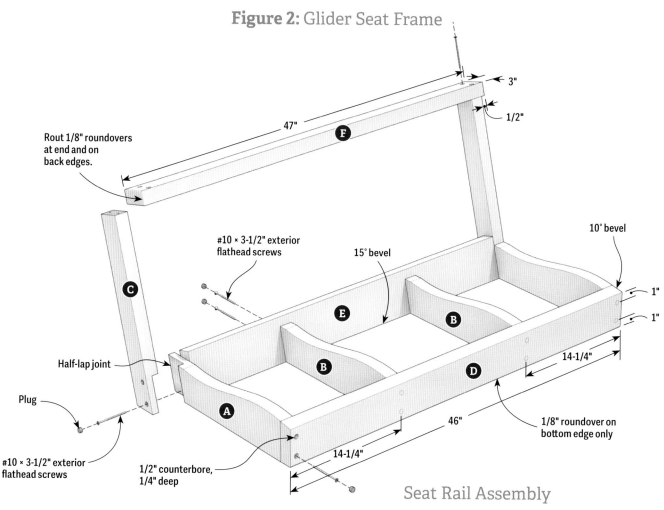

Rout 1/8" roundovers at end and on back edges.

47"

F

3"

1/2"

#10 × 3-1/2" exterior flathead screws

15° bevel

10° bevel

E

B

C

1"

1"

B

D

14-1/4"

Half-lap joint

Plug

A

46"

1/8" roundover on bottom edge only

#10 × 3-1/2" exterior flathead screws

1/2" counterbore, 1/4" deep

14-1/4"

Seat Rail Assembly

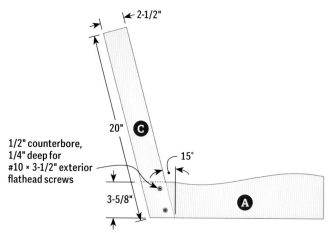

2-1/2"

20"

C

15°

1/2" counterbore, 1/4" deep for #10 × 3-1/2" exterior flathead screws

3-5/8"

A

then, using the clearance holes in the seat front rail as guides, drill pilot holes into the seat rail assemblies **(A/C)**. Drive screws to attach the seat front rail to the seat end assemblies.

5. Make the seat rear rail **(E)** by first bevel-ripping one edge of a piece of 1-1/2"-thick stock at 15°. Next, rip the piece to 4-3/4" wide. Now, crosscut the seat rear rail to the length listed in the **Cut List**.

6. Drill the countersunk clearance holes through the half-lap joints in the seat end assemblies **(A/C)**. With the beveled edge down, align the ends of the seat rear rail **(E)** with the front edge of the back supports **(C)** and drive the screws. Trim the middle seat rails **(B)** to fit, bore the needed holes, and screw them in place **(Figure 2)**, flush with the bottom edges of the seat front **(D)** and rear rails **(E)**.

Figure 3: Splats and Slats

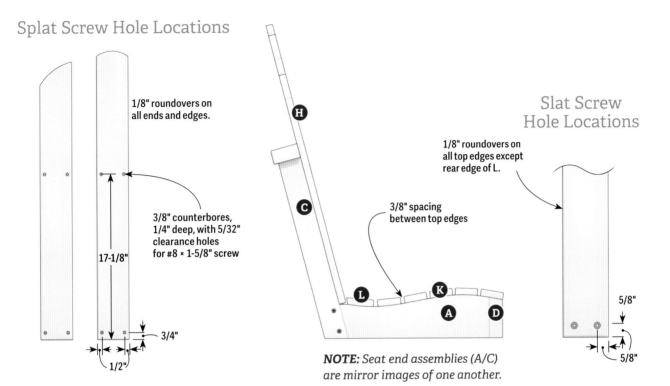

Splat Screw Hole Locations

1/8" roundovers on all ends and edges.

3/8" counterbores, 1/4" deep, with 5/32" clearance holes for #8 × 1-5/8" screw

17-1/8"

3/4"

1/2"

Slat Screw Hole Locations

1/8" roundovers on all top edges except rear edge of L.

3/8" spacing between top edges

5/8"

5/8"

NOTE: Seat end assemblies (A/C) are mirror images of one another.

7. Rip and crosscut the top seat rail **(F)** to size. Drill counterbores and clearance holes on the top face of the piece so they are centered on the back supports **(C)**. Note that the ends of the top seat rail extend 1/2" beyond each back support.

8. With your 1/8" roundover bit setup, rout the ends and rear edges of the top seat rail **(F)**. Do not rout the front edges.

9. Screw the top seat rail **(F)** to the seat assemblies **(A, C)**, with the front edges flush.

Make the back splats

1. Using 3/4"-thick stock, rip blanks to 3-1/2" wide for the back splats: center **(G)**, outer **(H)**, intermediate **(I)**, and middle **(J)**. Crosscut each blank at least 1" longer than its finished length in the **Cut List**.

2. Cut and adhere the copies of the two splat patterns **(Figure 9)** to one end of the appropriate blanks for the splats **(G, H, I, J)** **(Figure 3)**. Bandsaw to the waste side of the cutlines, and then disc-sand to the lines. Crosscut the parts to their final lengths. To form identical rounded and arched ends of the splats, use the flush-trimming technique in the sidebar (p. 72).

3. Mark the hole centers on the splats. Drill the counterbores and clearance holes.

4. Break the front ends and edges of the splats **(G, H, I, J)** with the 1/8" roundover bit.

5. Mark a centerline at the lower end of the center splat **(G)**. Cut scrap support strips to fit between the middle seat rails **(B)** and between the end **(A)** and middle **(B)** seat rails. Use double-faced tape or clamps to fix them to the seat rear rail **(E)** even with the top edges of the seat rails to serve as temporary rests.

Speedy Splat Shaping

There are a total of 11 back splats, and shaping each one from scratch takes time. By using an over-under flush-trim bit at the router table and a pattern template, you can achieve consistent results in short order.

Begin by adhering a paper copy of the rounded and curved patterns onto the ends of a piece of scrap 3/8" or 1/2" plywood having the same width as the splats. Carefully cut out and sand the ends of the plywood, making the routing template. Now cut a set of blanks for the splats, leaving the wood about 1" longer than the finished lengths in the **Cut List**. Using your template, pencil the appropriate shape on the ends of the blanks, and bandsaw just to the waste side of the cutline. With double-faced tape, attach the template to a splat blank, and flush-trim the curved edges as shown.

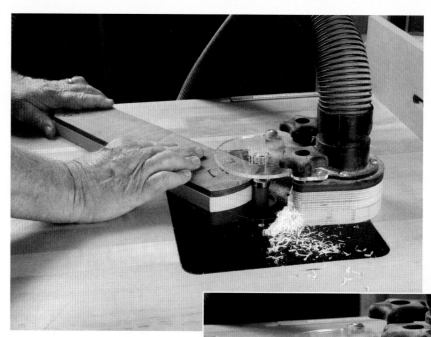

Flush-trim the ends of the slats using the bit (inset). Adjust the bit height, and flip the workpiece and template over as needed to rout with the grain to avoid end-grain tear out.

6. Next, make a mark on the center scrap strip at the midpoint of the bench assembly. Align the center splat mark with the strip mark, check that the center splat is square to the seat rear rail **(E)**, and drive screws to secure it to this rail and the top seat rail **(F)**.

7. Rest the bottom end of an outer splat **(H)** on the strip and, using spacers between the splats (mine were 3/4" thick), drive the screws to attach the slat to the rails **(E, F)**. Repeat the process to install the remaining splats. The edges of the outermost splats should be flush with the outside faces of the back supports **(C)**. Remove the support strips.

8. Glue plugs into all of the counterbores in the splat parts **(G, H, I, J)**. Then, flush the plugs to the surface with a plane or sanding block.

Cut the seat slats

1. Rip and crosscut the seat slats **(K)** and rear seat slat **(L)** to size. Note that the rear seat slat has a 15° bevel along its back edge **(Figure 2)**. Double-check that the slat lengths are flush to the sides of the bench assembly.

TIP: To ensure even splat spacing, subtract the total width of all the splats from the length between the outer faces of the back supports (C). Divide that number by 10. Use the resulting number to determine the needed thickness of your spacer.

2. Rout 1/8" roundovers on the upper edges of the seat slats **(K)**. Do not round over the back edge of the rear seat slat **(L)**.

3. Drill the counterbores and clearance holes in the slats (slat screw hole locations detail, **Figure 3**).

Figure 4: Arm Assembly (Right Arm Shown)

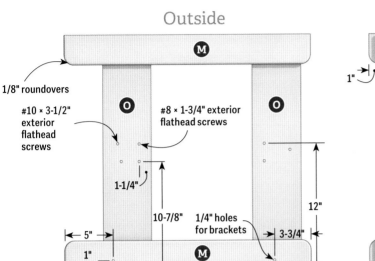

Outside

1/8" roundovers

#10 × 3-1/2" exterior flathead screws

#8 × 1-3/4" exterior flathead screws

1-1/4"

10-7/8"

1/4" holes for brackets

5"

1"

3-3/4"

12"

25-1/4"

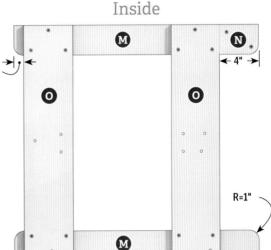

Inside

1"

4"

R=1"

NOTE: *1/2" counterbores, 1/4" deep for #10 screws 3/8" dia. counterbores, 1/4" deep for #8 screws*

4. Using a 3/8"-thick spacer between the slats and starting with the front seat slat **(K)**, screw all the slats in place. Leave a 1/4" space between the rear seat slat and back splats to allow for drainage. Be sure that the spacing between the slats appears the same.

5. Plug all the counterbores, and flush the plugs.

Make the arm assemblies

NOTE: *You'll make two arm assemblies that are mirror images of each other.*

1. Rip and crosscut the armrest rails **(M)** and armrest spacer **(N)**, referring to the **Cut List**. Glue and screw the spacer to the top armrest rail **(Figure 4)**. Mark and bandsaw the radiused ends; then sand them smooth.

2. Speed production by making the radius routing jig **(Figure 5)**. Then put it to work **(Photo C)**. As an alternative, you can bandsaw and sand the radii to final shape.

3. Rout roundovers along the edges and ends of the armrest rails **(M) (Figure 4)**. Do not rout the upper edge of the top rail.

4. Cut the armrest supports **(O)** to size.

5. To avoid confusion when marking hole locations, lay out the parts for the two mirror-image assemblies on your workbench. Drill the counterbores and holes in the rails (inside view, **Figure 4**). Then square and assemble the armrest rails **(M)** to the armrest supports **(O)** with an exterior glue and screws.

6. Plug the counterbores, and flush the plugs to the surface.

7. Drill the 1/4" holes for the glider brackets at your drill press to ensure that they are square to the surface.

8. Mark and drill counterbored holes (outside view, **Figure 4**). To ensure that the screws will find solid targets, dry-fit the arm assemblies on the seat assembly, as described in Step 9, to check the marked hole locations prior to drilling.

9. Stand the seat assembly on end to make it easier to attach the arm assemblies. Now make, and then clamp, a straightedge to an arm assembly, positioning it parallel to the bottom armrest rail **(M)** with its upper edge 10" above the bottom edge of the

Figure 5: Radius Routing Jig

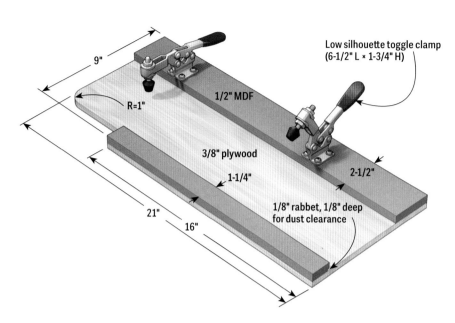

9"

R=1"

1/2" MDF

Low silhouette toggle clamp
(6-1/2" L × 1-3/4" H)

3/8" plywood

1-1/4"

2-1/2"

21"

16"

1/8" rabbet, 1/8" deep
for dust clearance

C

Round the ends. Clamp the workpieces in the radius routing jig and flush-trim the rough-cut radii for clean, consistent corners, guiding off the jig's smooth edge.

arm assembly. Place the appropriate arm assembly on the seat assembly **(Photo D)**. Locate the front edge of the forward armrest support **(O)** 1/4" past the front seat slat **(K)**. With the position confirmed, remove the arm assembly, apply glue to the mating surfaces, and reposition the assembly at the same location. Drill pilot holes, guiding off the counterbored holes, and drive the screws. Repeat the procedure for the other arm assembly.

Build the base

NOTE: You'll make two base end assemblies that are mirror images of each other.

1. Rip and crosscut the legs **(P)** and base rails **(Q)** to form the base end assemblies, referring to the **Cut List (Figure 6)**.

2. Chuck a 3/8" roundover bit into the table-mounted router; profile the edges and ends of the legs **(P) (Figure 6)**.

3. Mark the radii at the ends of the base rails **(Q)**, and then cut and smooth them. Rout a 1/8" roundover around the perimeter of the outer face of the base rails.

4. Mark the centers of the counterbores and holes in the base rails **(Q)**. Drill the counterbores and clearance holes, but not the glider brackets yet. Glue and clamp the base rails **(Q)** to the legs **(P)**, and then drive the screws. Glue in the plugs and flush them to the surface.

5. Take the completed base end assembly to your drill press, and drill the holes for the glider brackets.

6. Rip and crosscut the base stretchers **(R)**. Drill countersunk screw clearance holes into these parts **(Figure 6)**. (The fasteners will be hidden, so there's no need for counterbores.) Glue and screw the stretchers to the base end assemblies **(P/Q)**.

7. Measure between the base stretchers **(R)**, and use the dimension to cut the base spacers **(S)** to length. Screw the parts in place to further stabilize the base assembly, and check them for square.

Add the arms & hardware

NOTE: You'll make two arms that are mirror images of each other.

1. Cut the blanks for the arms **(T)** to size. Make a plywood pattern template using a copy of the arm pattern **(Figure 9)**. Drill the holes in

Figure 6: Base Assembly

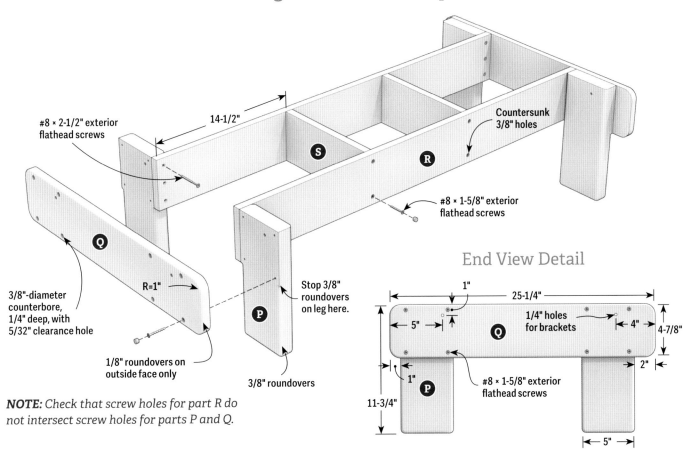

#8 × 2-1/2" exterior flathead screws

14-1/2"

Countersunk 3/8" holes

S

R

#8 × 1-5/8" exterior flathead screws

Q

3/8"-diameter counterbore, 1/4" deep, with 5/32" clearance hole

R=1"

P

Stop 3/8" roundovers on leg here.

1/8" roundovers on outside face only

3/8" roundovers

NOTE: *Check that screw holes for part R do not intersect screw holes for parts P and Q.*

End View Detail

1"

25-1/4"

1/4" holes for brackets

5"

Q

4"

4-7/8"

2"

1"

P

#8 × 1-5/8" exterior flathead screws

11-3/4"

5"

---

the plywood where indicated. Use the template to lay out the arms. Bandsaw the blanks. Adhere the template to one arm to flush-trim it and mark the holes **(Photo E)**. Flip the other arm and template and repeat. Remove the template.

2. Drill the counterbores and clearance holes in the arms **(T)**, where marked. Rout 1/8" roundovers along the perimeter on both faces.

3. Next, position the arm on the arm assemblies **(M/N/O)** and drive the screws **(Figures 1 and 7)**. Add the plugs and flush them.

D

Attach the arm assembly. Position the arm assembly on the seat assembly using the straightedge, and then use glue and drive screws of three different lengths to secure it.

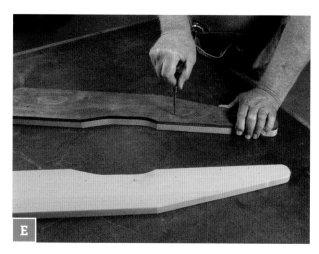

Mark the arms. Use a scratch awl to mark the holes in the arms, guiding off the 1/8" holes drilled in the plywood template.

Figure 7: Arm Detail

1/8" roundovers on top and bottom edges

Plug

#8 × 1-5/8" exterior flathead screw

3/8" counterbore, 1/4" deep

T

M

O

1/2"

1"

4. Attach the glider brackets to the base assembly **(Figure 8)**. Snug up the bolts, but don't overdo the torque.

5. Set the base assembly on a level surface, and make sure that it is oriented correctly—with the 2" projection of the base rails **(Q)** toward the front. Put the seat assembly in front of the base, and tilt it forward as you push the base assembly beneath it. Slide the two assemblies together to align them. (Or use a helper to set the seat on the base.)

6. Lift each end of the seat assembly, and place a 1/2"-thick spacer atop the base at each end to elevate the seat assembly. Align the holes in the seat assembly with the glider bracket, and install the hardware **(Photo F, Figure 8)**. Once you've installed the hardware, remove the spacers and check the glider's action.

Figure 8: Hardware Detail

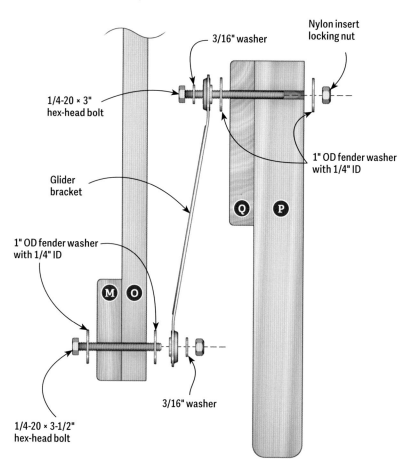

Nylon insert locking nut

3/16" washer

1/4-20 × 3" hex-head bolt

Glider bracket

1" OD fender washer with 1/4" ID

Q **P**

1" OD fender washer with 1/4" ID

M **O**

3/16" washer

1/4-20 × 3-1/2" hex-head bolt

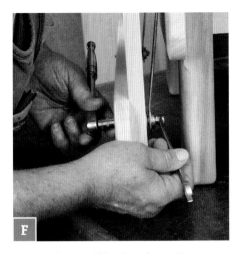

Assemble the glider brackets. Use a ratchet and wrench to snug up the bolts and nuts that attach the glider hardware.

TIP: Prevent the bottom leg ends of your glider from wicking up standing water by driving inexpensive nylon tack glides, elevating them off the ground. Avoid placing the glider on the grass, or the feet will rot.

7. Give the glider a test ride, and then remove the hardware so you can give the wood a final sanding with 220 grit. Wipe or blow off the dust and apply a finish. While you can go with a clear, exterior-grade finish with UV (ultraviolet) inhibitors, I chose buttermilk milk paint. After finishing, move the seat and base assemblies individually to a flat and level location where you intend to use the glider. Reattach the assemblies.

Adirondack Glider Supply & Cut List

	Part	Thickness	Width	Length	Qty.
A*	End seat rail	1-1/2"	4-9/16"	19"	2
B*	Middle seat rail	1-1/2"	4-9/16"	16-1/2"	2
C*	Back support	1-1/2"	2-1/2"	20"	2
D*	Seat front rail	1-1/2"	4-1/4"	46"	1
E	Seat rear rail	1-1/2"	4-3/4"	43"	1
F	Top seat rail	1-1/2"	3"	47"	1
G*	Center splat	3/4"	3-1/2"	22-7/8"	1
H*	Outer splat	3/4"	3-1/2"	25-1/4"	4
I*	Intermediate splat	3/4"	3-1/2"	29-5/8"	4
J*	Middle splat	3/4"	3-1/2"	30-3/4"	2
K	Seat slat	3/4"	2-1/2"	46"	5
L	Rear seat slat	3/4"	3"	46"	1
M	Armrest rail	3/4"	3"	25-1/4"	4
N	Armrest spacer	3/4"	3"	4"	2
O	Armrest support	3/4"	5"	23-1/2"	4
P	Leg	1-1/2"	5"	11-3/4"	4
Q	Base rail	3/4"	4-7/8"	25-1/4"	2
R	Base stretcher	3/4"	4-7/8"	41-3/4"	2
S	Base spacer	3/4"	4-7/8"	10-3/4"	2
T	Arm	3/4"	5-1/8"	27-3/4"	2
Supplies					
#8 exterior flathead screws				1-1/4"	
#8 exterior flathead screws				1-5/8"	
#8 exterior flathead screws				1-3/4"	
#8 exterior flathead screws				2-1/2"	
#10 exterior flathead screws				3-1/2"	
1/4-20 hex head machine screws				3"	4
1/4 hex head machine screws				3-1/2"	4
1/4" nylon insert locking nuts					
3/16" fender washers					
1/4" fender washers w/1" OD					
Glider brackets					4

Indicates that parts are initially cut oversized. See instructions.

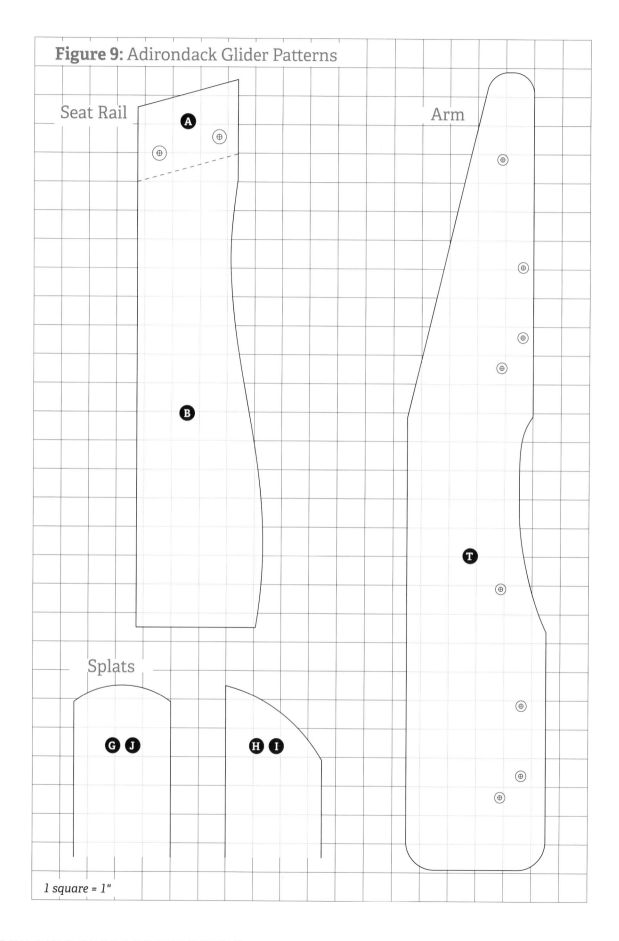

Figure 9: Adirondack Glider Patterns

Seat Rail

Arm

Ⓐ

Ⓑ

Ⓣ

Splats

Ⓖ Ⓙ

Ⓗ Ⓘ

1 square = 1"

Easy-Breezy Porch Swing

This simple-to-build project will be your go-to spot to sit and watch the world pass by.

By Jim Harrold

During the past two centuries, the country has witnessed porches come and go, and return again, for reasons of nostalgia and the pure love of sitting outdoors. And while benches, rockers, and wicker chairs help you relax in the open air, nothing offers more comfort than a porch swing. Indeed, it's as American as apple pie.

This traditional design, made from weather-resistant cypress, features a contoured seat and wide armrests for maximum relaxation. The seat support rails are extended beyond the armrests to keep the chains out of "arms" way. The porch swing hardware provides springs that offer a cushiony ride as you glide to and fro.

Err on the side of caution and purchase springs and chains that can bear more weight than you think you'll use, so there's no need to worry if an unexpected visitor hops on. Be sure to securely attach the hardware not only to the swing, but also the studs in the porch ceiling.

NOTE: *Our off-the-rack cypress measured .83" thick (a hair over 1-3/16"). Rather than needlessly feed wood to our planer, we used the stock as is. The extra thickness gave the seat and back assembly a little more heft, even though it did throw off a few of the measurements. If you decide to build this project from a harder wood, such as white oak or mahogany, you can use 3/4"-thick stock.*

Figure 1: Exploded View

Half-Lap Detail

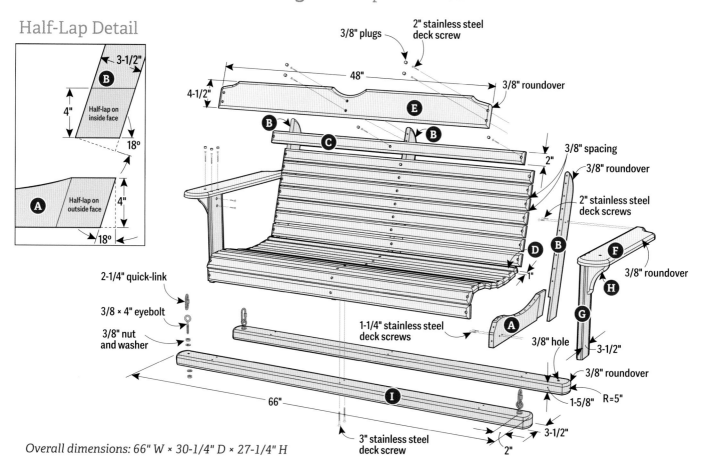

Overall dimensions: 66" W × 30-1/4" D × 27-1/4" H

Start with the seat/back assemblies

1. Rip a 6'-long board to 4" wide for the seat supports **(A)** and a 7'-long board to 3-1/2" for the back supports **(B)**. Cut each board into three equal lengths. (They are intentionally left a little long. You'll cut them to final length after joining the two together.) Set your table saw's miter gauge to 18° and cut one end of each seat and back support piece.

2. Lay out the locations of the half-lap joints on the angled ends of the seat and back supports **(A, B)** (half-lap detail, **Figure 1**). To find the shoulder line, lay one piece on top of the other, so that the mitered end of the top board is flush with the edge of the other, and draw on the bottom board. Rearrange the two boards so that the bottom board is on top and mark the other shoulder. Set a marking gauge to one-half the thickness of your stock and scribe a line along the edges and ends of both pieces.

3. Outfit your table saw with a 3/4" dado set. Adjust the height just shy of the scribed line. Using two pieces of scrap, make a test cut on the ends and check the fit. Continue raising the blade and retesting the cut until the stock faces are flush with each other and there is no offset between the two. Now cut the half-laps on the seat **(A)** and back **(B)** supports **(Photo A)**. Clean up the half-lap rabbets with a sanding block.

4. Apply exterior glue to the mating half-laps, and then clamp the pairs together to make three seat/back assemblies **(A/B)**. Let cure.

Cut half-laps. Cut the angled rabbets on the mating half-lap ends of the seat and back supports by first cutting along your cutline and then removing the waste.

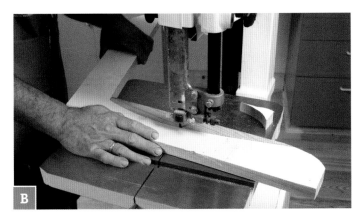

Cut just outside the line. Use a 1/4" blade in your bandsaw to cut along the outside edges of the pattern cutline to remove the waste. Later, sand the edges smooth.

Cut the curve in the crest rail. When cutting curves in long workpieces, such as the crest rail, a jigsaw is more convenient than a bandsaw. Clamp the workpiece to a solid table.

5. Enlarge the seat **(A)** and back support **(B)** patterns **(Figure 2)** to full-size and affix it to one of the seat/back assemblies **(A/B)**. Align the pattern's back and bottom edges with your wood. Saw to final shape along the front and top edges, cutting just outside the line **(Photo B)**.

6. Sand the seat/back assembly **(A/B)** to the line using disc and oscillating spindle sanders; strip off the pattern. Use this assembly as a pattern for the other two.

7. Clamp the three assemblies **(A/B)** together and sand and file as needed to make them identical. If necessary, use a rasp or sanding block to reestablish the two flat spots for the slats at the front of the seat as indicated on the pattern.

Make the slats, arms & rails

1. Referring to the **Cut List**, make 17 seat and back slats **(C)** and one transition slat **(D)**. With the hole-and-slat spacing jig (p. 82), mark the screw hole locations. Use a combination square to mark corresponding centered holes on the transition slat. Drill the 3/8"-wide × 5/16"-deep counterbored holes in the top faces of all slats. (You'll plug these later.)

2. Cut the crest rail **(E)**, arms **(F)**, arm supports **(G)**, and arm brackets **(H)** to the dimensions in the **Cut List**. Make copies of the crest rail center, arm, and bracket patterns **(Figures 3, 4, and 5)** and affix them to the corresponding parts.

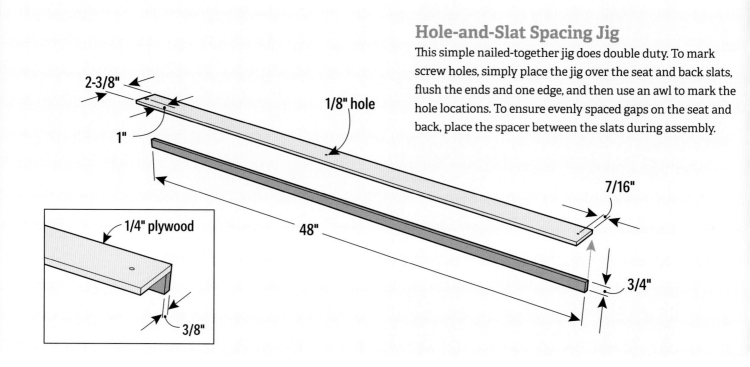

Hole-and-Slat Spacing Jig

This simple nailed-together jig does double duty. To mark screw holes, simply place the jig over the seat and back slats, flush the ends and one edge, and then use an awl to mark the hole locations. To ensure evenly spaced gaps on the seat and back, place the spacer between the slats during assembly.

3. Cut out the pattern shapes **(Photo C)**. Sand the edges to remove saw marks.

4. Selecting the straightest-grain stock, mill four pieces to 4" × 72". Glue the pieces in pairs, face to face. Once the glue dries, joint and cut the laminations to the final dimensions of 3-1/2" × 66" for swing support rails **(I)**. Mark the 1-3/4" radii at the ends and saw them to shape. Sand smooth.

NOTE: Depending on your stock, the rail's thickness may vary by 1/4". A thinner rail is more than strong enough to support the swing.

5. Round over the edges where shown with a router and 3/8" roundover bit **(Figure 1)**. Do not round over the part edges that join with other swing parts, such as where the edges of the seat/back assemblies **(A/B)** join slats **(C)**.

Assemble the swing

1. Set the seat/back assemblies **(A/B)** on the workbench, back edges down. Make a pair of scrapwood spacers so that, when clamped between the assemblies, the frame's total length is 48" and the middle assembly is centered at 24".

2. Position the crest rail **(E)** at the top ends of the back supports **(B)**, flush with the outside corners of the end cutouts. Use the rail's holes to mark and drill pilot holes in the edges of the seat/back assemblies. Drive the screws.

3. Use the hole-and-slat spacing jig for even spacing between the crest rail **(E)** and topmost slat **(C)**. Again,

to avoid splitting the wood, drill pilot holes in the seat/back assemblies **(A/B)** before driving the screws **(Photo D)**. Continue using the spacing jig to install the next seven slats.

4. Retrieve the arms **(F)**, brackets **(H)**, and arm supports **(G)** that you cut to shape earlier. Round over the parts **(Figure 1)**. Now, screw together two mirroring arm assemblies.

5. Set the swing assembly upright on the bench. (We rested it on a pair of straight 4×4s for ease of working.) Mark, drill, and screw the back ends of the arms **(F)** to the outside faces of the seat/back assemblies **(A/B)** **(Figure 1)**. Then, with the bottom ends of the arm supports **(G)** flush with the swing's bottom edge, glue and screw the arm assemblies **(F/G/H)** to the seat/back assemblies **(Photo E)**.

Attach the seat slats. Use the spacing jig to maintain an even 3/8" gap between slats. Attach the slats to the seat/back assembly with 2"-long stainless steel screws.

Attach the arm supports. Drill countersunk pilot holes through the seat/back assemblies and into the arm supports; then drive 1-1/2"-long stainless steel screws.

6. Attach the slats to the seat, starting at the front bottom edge of the seat/back assemblies **(A/B)** and working toward the back. Position the second and third slats on the flats prepared earlier. Use the spacing jig for the next six slats. Install the transition slat **(D)** when turning the inside corner of the seat.

TIP: Scribble a few lines across your stock before cutting your plugs. When they're cut free of the board, the lines will help you identify the small end so that you can correctly orient the plugs into the holes.

7. Using a drill press and tapered plug cutter, cut a batch of 3/8" plugs from leftover material. Apply glue to the inside walls of the counterbored screw holes using a small brush or nail head. Then tap the plugs into the holes **(Photo F)**. Trim the protruding plugs with a flush-cut saw and sanding block or block plane **(Photo F, inset)**.

Add the rails, hardware & finish

1. Place the swing support rails **(I)** parallel to each other on your workbench or assembly table and set the swing on top. Position the front rail so that it's directly below the arm supports **(G)**, and the back rail flush with the corner of the seat/back assemblies **(A/B)**. Center both rails from side to side, then make pencil lines indicating the locations of the seat/back assemblies. With a square, strike centerlines between each pair of marks across the rails.

2. Drill a pair of countersunk screw clearance holes up through the bottom face of the support rails **(I)** at each seat/back location.

3. Measure 2-1/4" in from the ends of the swing support rails **(I)** on the bottom faces. Strike an intersecting mark centered on the width of the rails. Using a drill press, drill 1" × 5/8"-deep counterbored recesses to conceal the eyebolt nuts and washers and 3/8" through holes through the rails for the bolt.

4. Add nuts and washers to 3/8" × 4" eyebolts, insert the eyebolts' threaded ends through the top faces of the rails, and secure to the rails with washers and nuts.

5. Reposition the support rails **(I)** to the bottom of the swing. Using the countersunk screw holes as guides, drill pilot holes centered on

Cutting Diagram

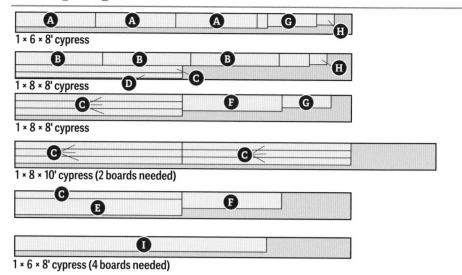

1 × 6 × 8' cypress

1 × 8 × 8' cypress

1 × 8 × 8' cypress

1 × 8 × 10' cypress (2 boards needed)

1 × 6 × 8' cypress (4 boards needed)

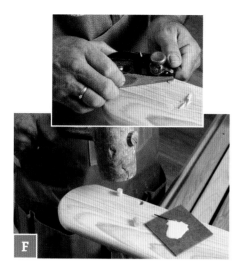

Insert the plugs. Apply glue and then tap the tapered plugs into the counterbored holes, aligning the grain. Trim the plugs with a flush-cut saw. Level them with a block plane or sanding block.

the bottom edges of the seat/back assemblies **(A/B)**. Drive the screws to fasten the rails to the swing.

6. Remove the hardware and finish-sand. Apply your choice of finish with a brush or by spraying. (Four coats of exterior water-based acrylic shown.)

7. Hang the swing to determine the height you want from the porch deck or ground using chain, springs, S-hooks, 3/8" × 4" eyebolts, 3/8" × 4" eyescrews (screwed into ceiling joists), and quick-links. Cut excess chain with bolt cutters or a hacksaw.

8. Reattach the hardware and go for a swing!

Porch Swing Supply & Cut List

	Part	Thickness	Width	Length	Qty.
A*	Seat support	3/4"	4"	23"	3
B*	Back support	3/4"	3-1/2"	25-1/8"	3
C	Seat/back slat	3/4"	2"	48"	17
D*+	Transition slat	3/4"	1"	48"	1
E	Crest rail	3/4"	4-1/2"	48"	1
F	Arm	3/4"	4-1/2"	28-1/4"	2
G	Arm support	3/4"	3-1/2"	14"	2
H	Arm bracket	3/4"	3"	5"	2
I	Swing support rail	1-5/8"	3-1/2"	66"	2
Supplies					
	3/8" stainless steel (SS) eyebolts			4"	4
	3/8" screw eyes			4"	2
	3/8" washers				8
	3/8" nuts				8
	#8 SS screws			2"	72
	#10 SS screws			1"	10
	#8 SS screws			3"	12
	Swing-Mate springs	2"	2"	8-1/2"	2
	Swing chain and ceiling hook hardware kit				

Indicates that parts are initially cut oversized. See instructions.

*+ The transition slat fits between the seat and back slats;
rip it to a width that maintains equal spacing.*

Figure 2: Seat and Seat Back Support Patterns
For full-sized pattern, enlarge by 400%

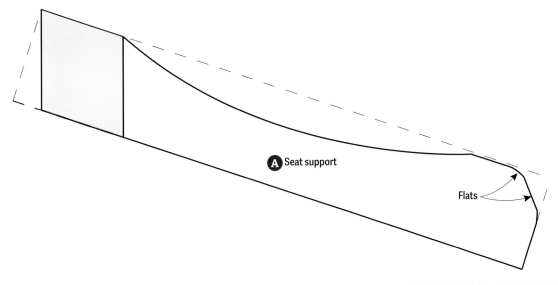

Back
support

B

How to Enlarge and Apply Paper Patterns

Paper patterns like those shown here save valuable shop time when building a project. Because of the sizes of the seat and back supports, crest rail, and arms, we include the patterns for these parts in reduced form. (The bracket is full sized.) To convert the reduced patterns to full size, you can go one of three ways:

If you have access to a copy machine, copy the curved portions of the pattern, such as the back end of the arm, to 200%. Place this enlarged pattern on the copy machine and copy it again at 200%. The resulting pattern will be enlarged by 400%, just what you need. For long curves, such as the seat support, make sequential copies and tape them together. The

total pattern length must equal the finished length of the part.

Take the pattern pages shown here to a local service that prints architectural blueprints and have them make you printed copies enlarged to 400%. This is your most expensive option.

Cut the full-sized patterns to shape and spray-adhere them to the respective project parts that you have cut to the finished lengths and widths in the **Cut List**. Using a bandsaw or jigsaw, cut the parts to final shape, just outside the cutlines. Finish-sand to the lines to remove saw marks. Then round over only those edges indicated in the Figures.

A Seat support

Flats

Figure 3: Crest Rail Center Pattern
For full-sized pattern, enlarge by 400%

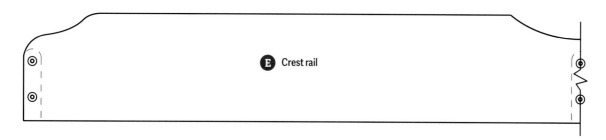

Figure 4: Arm Pattern
For full-sized pattern, enlarge by 400%

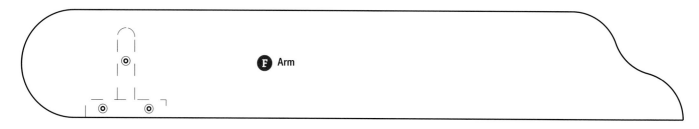

Figure 5: Bracket Pattern
Full-sized pattern

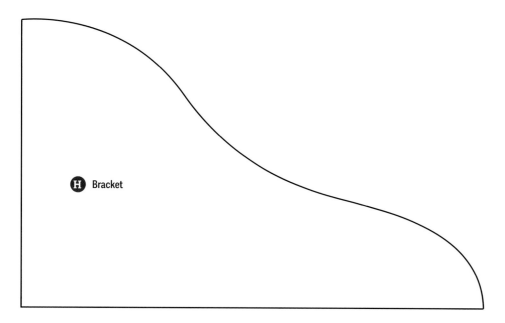

Build a Bench

A solid, simple bench made from two 2 × 10s offers the perfect place to sit.

By Joe Hurst-Wajszczuk

Some woodworkers turn up their noses at 2× lumber, but it's a great choice for beginners and for experienced woodworkers who want to enjoy a weekend in the shop. Cypress and cedar are nice, but considering that the pine version can be built for much less,

I'm betting that a few woodworkers may reconsider home center stock.

Despite its simplicity, this seat is surprisingly sturdy. Mortise-and-tenon construction and exterior-grade hardware create a base that's able to withstand almost anything Mother Nature might send its way.

Order of Work

1. Mill the wood.
2. Build the jigs.
3. Rout the mortises and tenons; assemble the legs.
4. Cut legs to final shape.
5. Dado the rails.
6. Assemble the base.
7. Attach the seat.

Figure 1: Exploded View

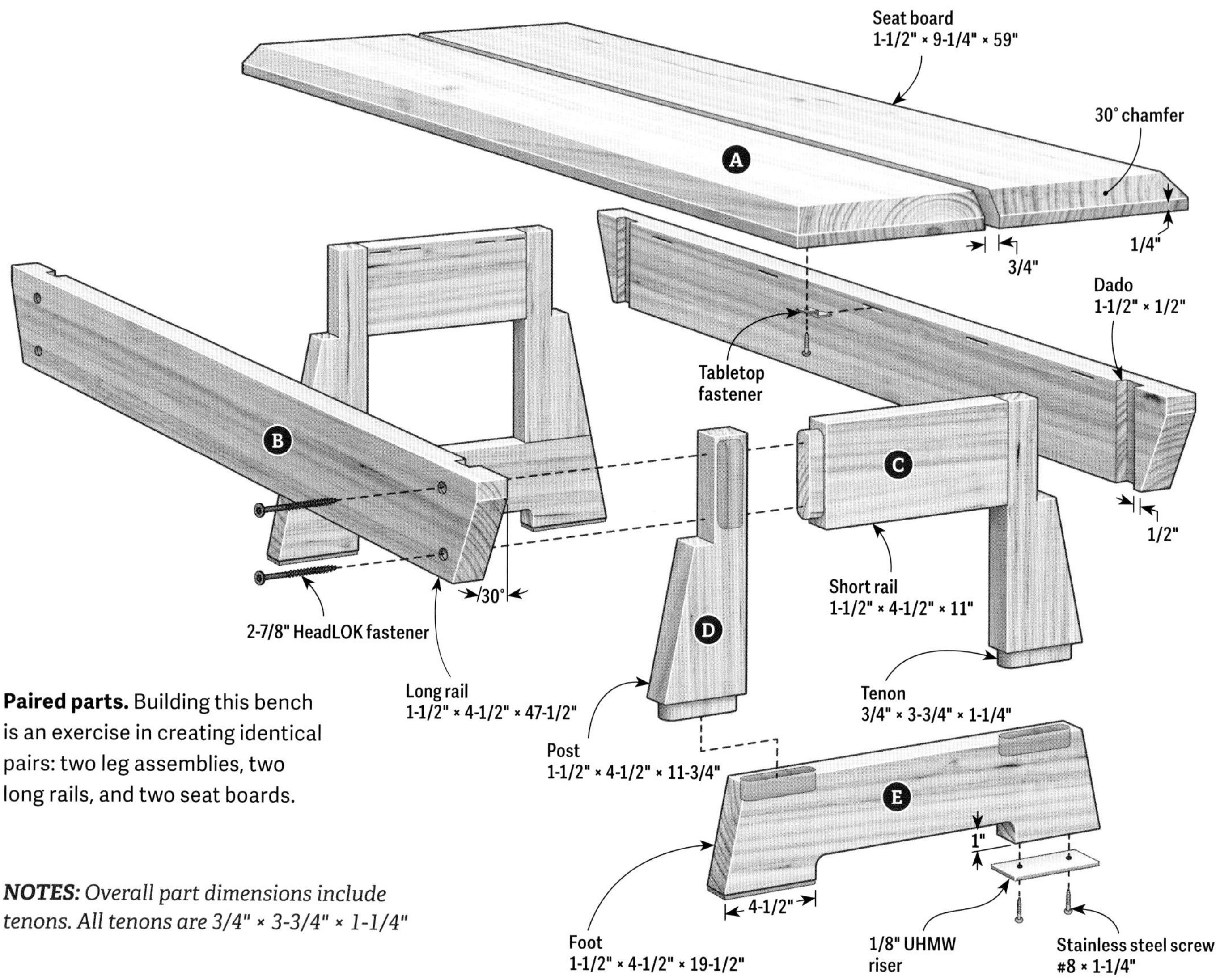

Seat board
1-1/2" × 9-1/4" × 59"

30° chamfer

Ⓐ

1/4"

3/4"

Dado
1-1/2" × 1/2"

Tabletop
fastener

1/2"

Ⓑ

Ⓒ

Short rail
1-1/2" × 4-1/2" × 11"

30°

Tenon
3/4" × 3-3/4" × 1-1/4"

2-7/8" HeadLOK fastener

Ⓓ

Long rail
1-1/2" × 4-1/2" × 47-1/2"

Post
1-1/2" × 4-1/2" × 11-3/4"

Ⓔ

1"

Paired parts. Building this bench
is an exercise in creating identical
pairs: two leg assemblies, two
long rails, and two seat boards.

4-1/2"

NOTES: *Overall part dimensions include
tenons. All tenons are 3/4" × 3-3/4" × 1-1/4"*

Foot
1-1/2" × 4-1/2" × 19-1/2"

1/8" UHMW
riser

Stainless steel screw
#8 × 1-1/4"

One quick hit to your home center, then start building

This project is designed to
make the most of two 2×10s.
To maximize yield, I outfitted my
table saw with a thin-kerf blade.
When planing, I stopped a few passes
sooner than I normally do and dealt
with deeper mill marks with a sander
and hand plane. Cutting parts to
rough length helps reduce milling,
but keep short pieces together so that
they can be machined safely. Should
your stock come in under the listed
dimensions, it's no big deal, but center
the mortising jig on your stock.

The mortise-and-tenon leg
assemblies are joined with Titebond
III. The table clips do more than
create a cleaner-looking seat; they
eliminate the screw holes that might
let in moisture or cause rust stains.

It might seem out of sequence,
but I suggest varnishing the seat
before starting the leg assemblies.
This way, these boards will be a few
protective coats ahead of the game
when you start to finish the base.

Make the legs, then rout & cut them to shape

The joinery goes quickly, thanks to a few shop-made jigs. I made this dedicated T-shaped jig for the mortises, and then used my router table to cut the matching tenons. I put the bit/bushing setup into service again when routing the lift on the bottom of the leg assembly.

To cut the tapered sides, first lay out the sides on the assembled leg assemblies. Next, set the leg **(D)** on a plywood sled, and set stopblocks so that the line corresponds to the edge. Finally, cut the notches for the rails.

Tenon & Mortise Tune-Up

Rounding tenons. Rounding the ends of the tenons is faster and easier than squaring the ends of the mortises. Plane the cheeks as needed for a snug fit.

Chisel a chamfer. Chamfering the top edges makes it easier to fit the tenons and catches excess glue that would otherwise ooze from the joint.

Figure 2: Mortising Template

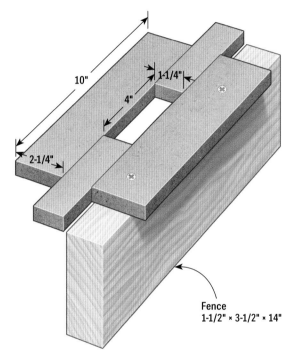

10"
1-1/4"
4"
2-1/4"

Fence
1-1/2" × 3-1/2" × 14"

A

Taking the plunge. When paired with a plunge router equipped with a 1/2" upcut spiral bit and 1" OD bushing, this simple MDF jig makes quick work of the mortises in the feet and posts. Plan on vacuuming out the cavity a few times before completing the mortise.

B

Slide to the stop. Cutting the 1-1/4" long tenons on the router table takes several passes, but results in super-smooth cheeks. Attach a fence and stopblock to your miter gauge as shown.

Figure 3: Leg Assembly

Figure 4: Foot Template

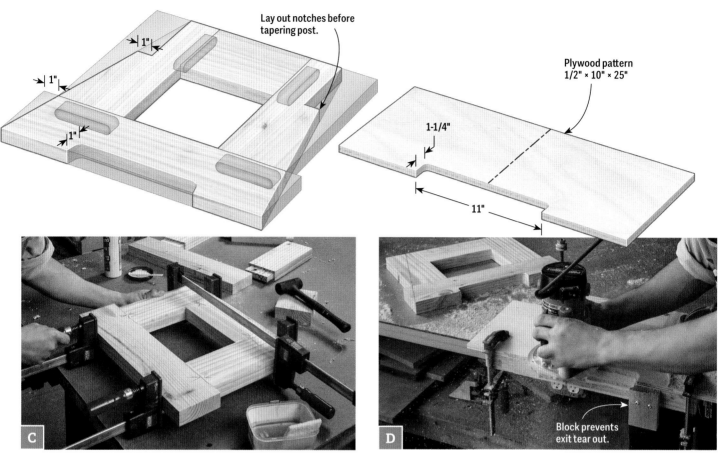

Lay out notches before tapering post.

1"

1"

1"

Plywood pattern
1/2" × 10" × 25"

1-1/4"

11"

C

D

Block prevents exit tear out.

Squeeze it together. Three clamps are all it takes to join the leg assemblies. Make sure that the foot extends past the outer edges of both posts by 1".

Follow the pattern. The lift for the foot can be done with a bandsaw or jigsaw, but the bit and bushing combo produces a curve that requires less cleanup. Tack a block to the foot to prevent tear out.

E

Use a sled to slice the leg. This plywood sled produces perfectly symmetrical sides without picking up a protractor. After cutting one edge of each leg assembly, adjust the side stopblock and cut the opposite edge. Cut the rail notches with a handsaw or jigsaw.

Bench Supply & Cut List

	Part	Thickness	Width	Length	Qty.
A	Seat board	1-1/2"	9-1/4"	59"	2
B	Long rail	1-1/2"	4-1/2"	47-1/2"	2
C	Short rail	1-1/2"	4-1/2"	11"	2
D	Post	1-1/2"	4-1/2"	11-3/4"	4
E	Foot	1-1/2"	4-1/2"	19-1/2"	2
Supplies					
	UHMW riser	1/8"	1-1/2"	4-1/2"	4
	#8 stainless steel screws			1-1/4"	8
	HeadLOK fastener			2-7/8"	4
	Table clips				10

Assemble the base & add the seat

After cutting the long rails **(B)** to length, lay out the dadoes. To make perfectly matching dadoes, I again enlisted my plunge router and spiral bit (but removed the bushing guide), and clamped both rails to a T-square jig, as shown at right. To join the long rails **(B)** to the leg assemblies **(C/D/E)**, I used exterior-grade structural screws that sport special threads and tough epoxy finish.

This bench isn't going to come apart at the seams, but a few extra steps can help keep it looking good.

To seal and protect the wood, I disassembled and applied three coats of spar varnish to all surfaces. Lastly, I attached UHMW foot pads to protect base from standing water.

Two rails in one pass. To create matching dadoes in both long rails, simply align the notch in the jig's crossbar with your layout line and rout. Repeat on the opposite end. A scrap board prevents chip-out.

Lock in the rails. Epoxy-coated structural HeadLOK screws offer the strength of a bolt, but can be installed with a drill or impact driver. The head is designed to self-sink; for a cleaner appearance, counterbore the holes with a 3/8" Forstner bit.

Now clip in the seat. Use a biscuit joiner to cut #10 biscuit slots in the long and short rails. The fasteners hold the seat to the base, but allow the wood to respond to seasonal changes in humidity.

BYOB (Build Your Own Bench)

The simplicity and low cost of this project should encourage you to take creative license. For example, if you plan on using this bench in a garage or three-season porch, try painting the base with milk paint and topping it with Watco Danish Oil. For outdoor use, step up to spar varnish. Although a thermo-treated poplar seat costs more than construction-grade pine, this walnut imposter is weather and insect resistant.

Garden Bench

Outdoor materials and sound joinery make
this a bench that will last generations.

By Andy Rae

Spring is in the air, and it's time to spend some quality time outside—sitting down, of course! To serve this purpose, why not make a great outdoor bench that you can "plant" in the garden or on a patio? This classically inspired bench is fun to make, and it's constructed using a weather-resistant wood.

We chose cypress, because it's inexpensive, readily available, and known for its weather resistance. Other insect- and decay-resistant woods include redwood and cedar.

For solid joinery, we chose mortise and tenon. To build your skill set, we'll show how to mill the mortises with a router and a pair of edge guides, but

you can also use a benchtop mortiser or employ a loose-tenon routing jig to bore the mortise half of the joint. You can use a jig on both mating parts of the joint and replace the more time-eating traditional tenon with a loose one. As long as your joints fit snugly, nobody—not even your bench—will detect the difference.

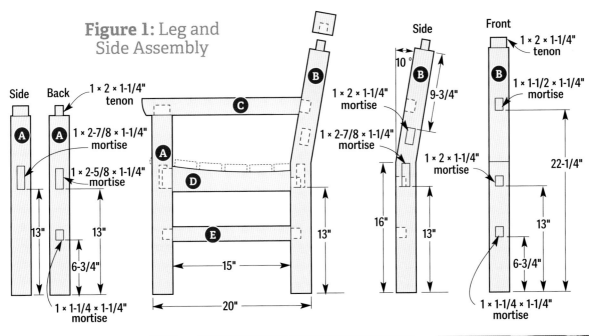

Figure 1: Leg and Side Assembly

Side   Back   1 × 2 × 1-1/4" tenon

1 × 2-7/8 × 1-1/4" mortise

1 × 2-5/8 × 1-1/4" mortise

13"   13"

6-3/4"

1 × 1-1/4 × 1-1/4" mortise

15"

20"

13"

Side

10°

9-3/4"

1 × 2 × 1-1/4" mortise

1 × 2-7/8 × 1-1/4" mortise

1 × 2 × 1-1/4" mortise

16"   13"

Front

1 × 2 × 1-1/4" tenon

1 × 1-1/2 × 1-1/4" mortise

22-1/4"

13"

6-3/4"

1 × 1-1/4 × 1-1/4" mortise

Draw out assembly diagram.
Avoid errors with a full-sized side assembly drawing containing pattern measurements and angles.

Apply the back leg template. Use the leg template to lay out the back legs. Align the template with a straight edge of the stock.

Saw the leg. Keep the leg front against the fence. Stop the saw when the blade touches the bottom inside corner.

Start with stock prep

1. Face-glue 6/4 boards to create stock thick enough to make parts A–J **(Cut List)**. Use a foam roller to spread the glue evenly, then space clamps to ensure uniform pressure over the boards.

2. Plane the front legs **(A)**, back legs **(B)**, and crest rail **(I)** to 2-1/2" thick. Continue planing the arms **(C)**, side seat rails **(D)**, front seat rail **(F)**, back seat rail **(G)**, center seat rail **(H)**, and lower back rail **(J)** to 2" thick.

Plane the stretchers **(E)** to 1-3/4" thick. (Note that the stock for the back legs **(B)** needs to be 6" wide).

Leave the back legs **(B)** over-width, but cut the rest of the parts to the finished sizes. Leave the arms **(C)** and crest rail **(I)** square for now.

3. Thickness enough 5/4 stock to make three 7/8"-thick back slats **(K)** and six seat slats **(M, N)**. Finally, thickness 6/4 stock to make ten 1-1/4"-thick back posts **(L)**. Leave these parts oversized for now; trim

them to final width and length after assembling the bench frame.

Make the leg

1. Make a full-sized drawing for the side on a piece of 1/4"-thick plywood **(Figure 1, Photo A)**. Include all the joinery. The drawing makes it easier to lay out the joints and measure the sloping angle at the bench back.

2. Make a pattern for the back legs **(B)** using another piece of 1/4" plywood. Bandsaw or jigsaw the pattern and

D

Rout leg mortises. Do two passes using a handheld router and straightedge attachment, registering the edge guide on both faces to ensure that the mortise is centered on the stock.

Figure 2: Slat and Post Locations

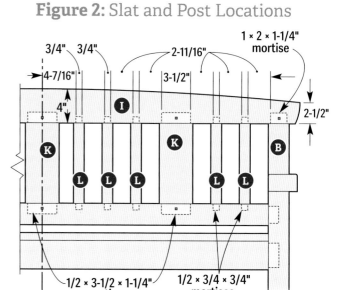

3/4"   3/4"   2-11/16"

1 × 2 × 1-1/4" mortise

4-7/16"

3-1/2"

2-1/2"

4"

I

K   **K**   **B**

L   **L**   **L**   **L**   **L**

1/2 × 3-1/2 × 1-1/4" mortises

1/2 × 3/4 × 3/4" mortises

E

Square the mortises. Use a chisel on the rounded ends of your mortises. Marking the mortise depth on the chisel's back is an easy way to gauge your progress.

F

Rout seat rail mortises. Clamp a scrap straightedge over both front and back seat rails to rout the cross-grain mortises.

G

Cut tenons. With a dado sled and stopblock, you can cut tenons on long pieces with control and precision.

smooth its edges with sandpaper. Use the pattern to draw the shape of the leg onto the leg stock **(Photo B)**.

3. Cut the back legs **(B)** to rough shape on the bandsaw, staying about 1/16" outside the pencil line. Use a stationary belt sander or hand plane to work up to your line on the front of the leg.

NOTE: Save the wedge-shaped offcuts. You'll use them as clamping cauls during assembly.

4. Using your table saw, set the rip fence to 2-1/2", raise the blade to full height, and trim the rear face of the back leg **(Photo C)**. Stop when the forward-most part of the blade—the teeth closest to the tabletop—touches the intersecting angle. Carefully turn off the saw, then flip the leg end-to-end and make a second cut in similar fashion.

NOTE: When making stopped cuts on the table saw, keep the workpiece firmly against the fence as you turn

off the saw. Make certain that the blade has come to a complete stop before flipping the workpiece.

Remove the remaining ridge from the inside corner with a chisel. Smooth all the faces with 150-grit sandpaper.

Cut mortises & tenons

1. Lay out and cut the mortises in the legs **(A, B)**, arms **(C)**, seat rails **(F, G)**, crest rail **(I)**, and lower back rail **(J)** (refer to the spacing in **Figure 1** and the slat and post mortise layout

Figure 3: Exploded View

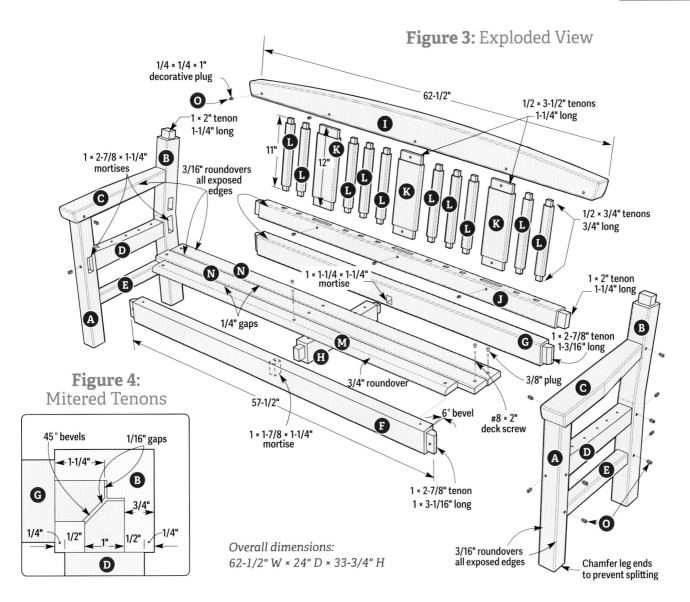

1/4 × 1/4 × 1"
decorative plug

O

1 × 2" tenon
1-1/4" long

1 × 2-7/8 × 1-1/4"
mortises

B

3/16" roundovers
all exposed
edges

62-1/2"

1/2 × 3-1/2" tenons
1-1/4" long

11"

12"

I

L **K** **L** **L** **L** **K** **L** **L** **K** **L** **L** **L**

1/2 × 3/4" tenons
3/4" long

C

D

E

A

N **N**

1 × 1-1/4 × 1-1/4"
mortise

1/4" gaps

J

1 × 2" tenon
1-1/4" long

B

1 × 2-7/8" tenon
1-3/16" long

G

3/8" plug

C

Figure 4:
Mitered Tenons

45° bevels   1/16" gaps

1-1/4"

B

G

3/4"

1/4"   1/2"   1"   1/2"   1/4"

D

57-1/2"

1 × 1-7/8 × 1-1/4"
mortise

M

H

3/4" roundover

F

6° bevel

#8 × 2"
deck screw

1 × 2-7/8" tenon
1 × 3-1/16" long

Overall dimensions:
62-1/2" W × 24" D × 33-3/4" H

A

D

E

O

3/16" roundovers
all exposed edges

Chamfer leg ends
to prevent splitting

in **Figure 2**). To cut the 1"-wide mortises in all the parts, except the seat rails **(F, G)**, I used a handheld router, a 1/2" upcut spiral bit, and a commercial edge guide. Set the fence to rout one-half of the mortise, then turn the stock around, register the guide against the opposite side of the stock, and rout the second half **(Photo D)**. Square the double-rounded ends with a chisel **(Photo E)**.

2. Mortise in the front and back seat rails **(F, G)** by clamping both

rails together and then clamping a straightedge made from a piece of 3/4" MDF or plywood across the stock **(Photo F)**. Reset the straightedge after the first cut to complete the 1"-wide mortises. Use a chisel to square off the rounded ends of the mortises.

3. Lay out the tenons to match your mortises **(Figures 1, 3, 4, and 5)**. Note that the tenons on the front **(A)** and back **(B)** legs are mirror images of each other; make sure you lay them out correctly before cutting.

4. Use your table saw and a dado blade to cut the tenons on the front legs **(A)**, back legs **(B)**, side seat rails **(D)**, stretchers **(E)**, front seat rails **(F)**, back seat rails **(G)**, center seat rails **(H)**, and lower back rail **(J)**. To do this tenon work, you can use a jig or simply lay the stock flat on the table saw and use a crosscut sled to carry the parts over the dado blade **(Photo G)**.

5. Cut the tenons on the angled back legs **(B)**. Depending on your saw, you may be able to switch from the

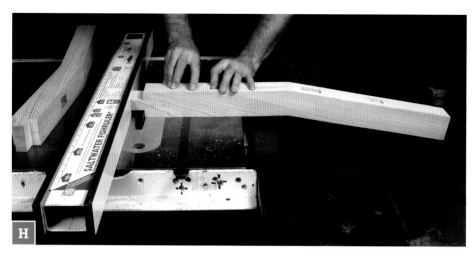

H

I

Cut the tenon. Hanging the leg over the side of the saw will enable you to cut the tenon cheeks on the back leg and allow the table to carry the weight of the leg.

Mark the inner face of the miter. Insert the tenon into the mortise and draw a line as shown.

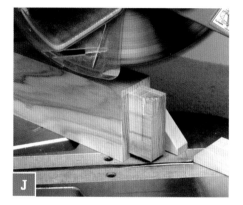

J

K

Miter the tenon. Set the saw to 45° and miter the end of the tenon just past the pencil line.

Cut the shoulder. Use the table saw's miter gauge to cut the 10° shoulder, setting the end of the arm against the fence.

sled to the miter gauge and let the stock hang down over the side of the table saw **(Photo H)**. If making the cut as shown is impossible without removing your table saw's wing, you may decide to use a tenoning jig.

6. The tenons on the stretchers **(E)**, front seat rail **(F)**, and back seat rail **(G)** are mitered so that they can remain as long as possible **(Figures 3 and 4)**. To do this, dry-fit each square-ended tenon into its respective

mortise and mark where the inner mortise wall meets the face of the tenon **(Photo I)**. Set the miter saw to 45° and trim the end of each tenon, cutting on or just past your marked line **(Photo J)**. Overcutting the miter by 1/16" ensures that the tenons don't hit when you assemble the bench.

7. Cut a 10° miter on the ends of the arms **(C)** using the miter saw. Now, using your table saw and miter gauge set for a 10° cut, saw one

shoulder, then reset the gauge to 10° in the opposite direction and saw the opposing shoulder **(Photo K)**.

8. Attach a 10° fence screwed to a tenoning jig and cut the tenon's cheeks **(Photo L)**. Set the rip fence to desired tenon thickness; make two rip cuts for each arm.

NOTE: Remove most of the waste with a handsaw to prevent the risk of offcuts getting caught between the jig and blade and flying backward at the end of the cut.

9. Lay out the width of the tenons and make these cuts on the bandsaw **(Photo M)**. Finally, crosscut the shoulders with a handsaw. Use a chisel to clean up any inside corners.

Cut the angled & curved parts

1. Bevel the top edge of the front seat rail **(F)** by angling the table

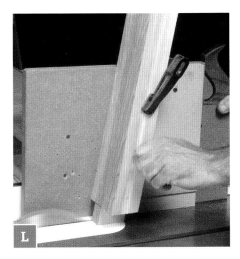

Rip the tenon. Set up a 10° fence on a jig to rip the tenon cheeks. Remove the bulk of the waste with a handsaw to avoid kickback.

Bandsaw the tenons to width. Finish the short shoulders with a fine-tooth handsaw.

Mark the crest rail curve. Clamp a piece of curved stock to the face of the crest rail and draw the curve onto the stock.

saw blade to 6°. Be sure to orient the rail so the bevel slopes toward the back of the seat **(Figure 3)**.

2. Draw the curve on one arm **(C)**, the crest rail **(I)**, and one side seat rail **(D)** using a pliable stick of straight-grained wood to draw the curve. (I made my "fairing stick" from leftover ash and attached a piece of string to one end to hold the curve.) Bend the stick into the desired curve, then tie off the opposite end of the stick. Position the stick to mark on your stock, clamp it, and draw the curve **(Photo N)**.

3. Using the patterns **(Figures 6 and 7)**, make a full-scale template of the ends of the arm **(C)** and crest rail **(I)** from 1/4" plywood. Use the template to draw the curves on the stock. Now saw the curves on the arms **(C)**, crest rail **(I)**, and seat rails **(D, H)** using the bandsaw or jigsaw. (Save the long offcut from the crest

rail **(I)**; you'll use it as a clamping caul during the assembly process.)

TIP: When making parts with curves, such as the arms and seat rails, saw and smooth out one part, then use it as a guide for its mate.

4. Smooth the curves on the arms **(C)** and crest rail **(I)** with a sanding block or hand plane, taking light cuts and feeling for a continuous curve with your fingers. The concave curve of the seat rails **(D, H)** is hidden under the seat slats, so smoothing this area isn't very important. I used an oscillating spindle sander on the curved areas, which removed most of the saw marks.

5. Refine the ends of the arms **(C)** and crest rail **(I)** using a spindle sander or 150-grit sandpaper wrapped around a wood block. Check that the curve is true by nesting the pattern you made earlier against the rail's end **(Photo O)**.

Measure & fit the back

1. Rather than rely solely on the **Cut List**, dry-assemble the frame and measure between the crest rail **(I)** and lower back rail **(J) (Photo P)**. To your measurement, add 2-1/2" for the 1-1/4"-long tenons on both ends the back slats **(K)** and 1-1/2" for the pair of 3/4"-long tenons on the back posts **(L)**. Go ahead and cut the slats and posts to finished length.

NOTE: The tenons on the posts are shorter than the slats to ease assembly. This lets you connect the crest rail to the three back slats before lining up and connecting the 10 posts. Trying to position 13 tenons all at once in a single glue-up is asking for trouble.

2. Using a table saw with a dado set and a miter gauge (or the dado sled shown in **Photo G**), cut the tenons on the back slats **(K)** and back posts **(L) (Photo Q)**.

Smooth the ends. Use the plywood pattern to check your progress as you refine the curve on the ends of the crest rail.

Take exact measurements. Dry-fit the bench, then measure the distance between the crest rail and the lower back rail with a rule to obtain the exact length of the slats and posts, including the tenons.

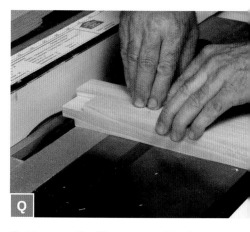

Cut tenons. Position a scrap block behind the slats and posts to ensure clean, tear out–free cuts on the front and back faces of your workpieces. Use your miter gauge to make the cut.

Figure 5: Angled and Curved Parts

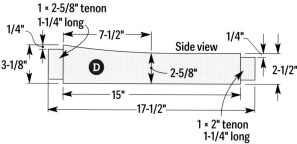

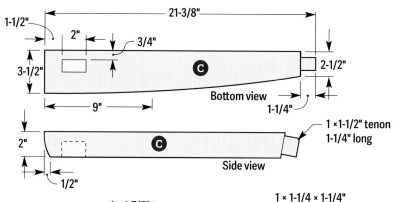

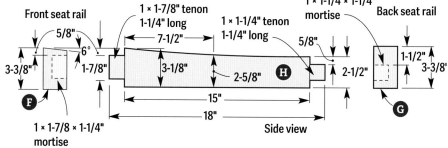

3. Round over all sharp edges. I used a 3/16"-roundover bit chucked in a table-mounted router and routed all the accessible edges. For those areas where the bit can't reach, use a block plane or a rasp to knock off the corner, then smooth the curve with 150-grit sandpaper.

TIP: If you need to reduce the size of a seat slat, rip or shave a smaller amount from two or three slats. It's less obvious than ripping it all off one slat.

Assemble the frame & the back

1. Starting with a side assembly, brush glue into the mortises in the legs **(A, B)** and onto the tenons on the arms **(C)**, seat rail **(D)**, and stretcher **(E)**. Press the parts together by hand and close the joints with clamps. Use the wedges you saved

earlier to help with clamping the angled back leg **(Photo R)**.

2. Glue and square the center seat rail **(H)** to the front and back seat rails **(F, G)**. When dry, attach the rails to one side assembly, making sure that the shoulders on both rails seat snugly against the legs. Add the lower

Assemble the sides first. Use the leg offcuts to keep the clamp square to the work. Remove excess glue in the open mortises.

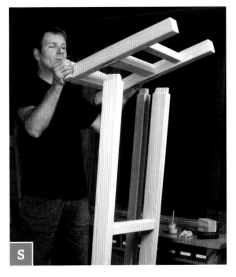

Attach the frame. Join the two side assemblies to the seat rails and lower back rail, gluing the joints and clamping the frame square.

Install the back slats. Tap home all the back slats and posts, then cap them and the back legs with the crest rail. Use your curved offcuts for good clamp purchase, taping them in place as shown.

back rail **(J)**, join the remaining side assembly, and then pull it together with clamps **(Photo S)**. Set the assembly aside to dry, but before you do, add the crest rail **(I)**—without glue—to the back legs **(B)** to help keep the frame square while the glue sets.

3. Add the back slats **(K)** and back posts **(L)**, then cap it with the crest

rail **(I)**. Work quickly, so that the glue doesn't have a chance to set up before bringing all the joints home. Use the curved offcuts you saved earlier to protect the crest rail and as a clamping aid, tapping the joint home **(Photo T)**. Add decorative pegs to the mortise-and-tenon joints if you wish. (See p. 101.)

Add the seat

1. Double-check the fit of the seat slats **(M, N)** on your bench, then cut them to length. Next, set up your drill press with a countersink/counterbore bit and drill the slats for #8 coated deck screws and 3/8" plugs. Soften the edges and ends of all the seat slats, but rout a larger radius on the front seat slat **(M)** to take off the edge and make the curve more thigh-friendly **(Figure 3)**.

2. Attach the seat slats with #8 deck screws. To maintain consistent slat spacing, use 1/4"-thick spacers during installation.

3. Chuck a 3/8" tapered plug cutter into your drill press and cut matching plugs using some leftover project scrap. Tap the face-grain plugs into the holes with glue, carefully orienting the grain of the plug in line with the grain of the slats. Once the glue has dried, saw the plugs flush with the seat using a flush-trimming saw. Finish up by sanding the plugs smooth with 150-grit sandpaper wrapped around a block of wood or using a paring chisel.

Cutting Diagram

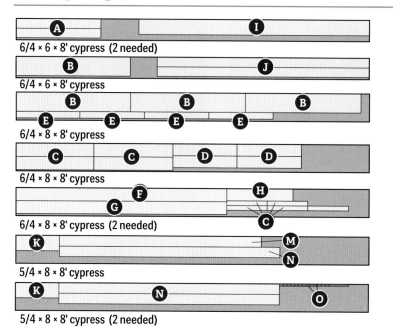

6/4 × 6 × 8' cypress (2 needed)

6/4 × 6 × 8' cypress

6/4 × 8 × 8' cypress

6/4 × 8 × 8' cypress

6/4 × 8 × 8' cypress (2 needed)

5/4 × 8 × 8' cypress

5/4 × 8 × 8' cypress (2 needed)

Garden Bench Supply & Cut List

	Part	Thickness	Width	Length	Qty.
A	Front leg	2-1/2"	2-1/2"	23-1/4"	2
B	Back leg	2-1/2"	2-1/2"	31-1/4"	2
C	Arm	2"	3-1/2"	21-3/8"	2
D	Side seat rail	2"	3-1/8"	17-1/2"	2
E	Stretcher	1-3/4"	1-3/4"	17-1/2"	2
F	Front seat rail	2"	3-3/8"	57-1/2"	1
G	Back seat rail	2"	3-3/8"	57-1/2"	1
H	Center seat rail	2"	3-1/8"	18"	1
I	Crest rail	2-1/2"	4"	62-1/2"	1
J	Lower back rail	2"	2-1/2"	57-1/2"	1
K	Back slat	7/8"	4"	12"	3
L	Back post	1-1/4"	1-1/4"	11"	10
M	Front seat slat	7/8"	2-3/4"	55"	1
N	Seat slat	7/8"	2-3/4"	60"	5
O	Peg	1/4"	1/4"	1-1/2"	25
	Supplies				
	#8 deck screws			2"	

All parts initially cut oversized. See instructions for further details.

A Square Peg for a Round Hole

Thanks to modern adhesives, pegging a joint is usually unnecessary. I like pegs because they look great, especially the square ones. Most of the pegs are less than 1"-long.

After laying out the peg locations, use a 1/4" chisel (I used a hollow chisel from my mortiser—without the inner bit), striking it firmly enough to create a 1/4"-deep hole. Next, drill through the square hole with a 1/4" twist bit 1/2" deep. Wrap a piece of tape around your bit to flag the correct depth.

Rip some stock 1/4"-square, then cut pegs **(O)** about 1-1/2" long. To make the pegs easier to set, drill a shallow divot with a countersink bit into a block of hardwood. Place the peg in the divot and tap it with a hammer to compress-bevel the corners.

Spread glue on the beveled end of the peg and drive that end into the hole, lining up the square edges with the edges of the hole. Thanks to cypress' relative softness, the hole will compress to accommodate the edges of the peg, leaving a square peg in a round hole. Once the glue has set, trim the protruding peg flush and sand smooth.

Figure 6: Crest Rail End Template

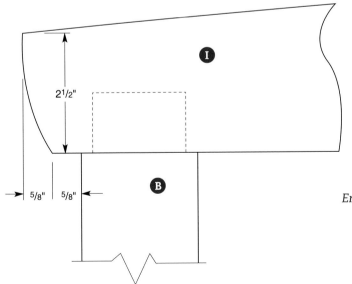

Figure 7: Arm End Template

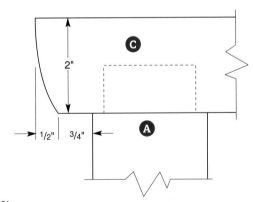

Enlarge 200%

Potting Bench

Get ready for planting season with this
easy-to-make garden center.

By Ken Burton

You don't need a green thumb to appreciate that a potting bench is as much of a necessity to a gardener as a workbench is to a woodworker. For starters, a potting bench provides a comfortable work surface, enabling gardeners to tend seedlings and repot plants without having to work on their hands and knees. A good bench also keeps supplies, such as potting soil, pots, garden tools, and fertilizers, in one convenient location, so that gardeners can make the most of their green time.

The design shown here does all that in spades, combining form with function. In addition to its elegantly-arched aprons, it features a segmented work surface with three removable panels. Two of the panels are slotted, making cleanup a simple matter of brushing leftover soil into the bins below.

Construction is downright easy: basic butt and miter joints, a few rabbets and dadoes, followed by assembly with screws. You can build the bench in one or two weekends and make gardening easier for many seasons to come. Thermo-wood (poplar) and exterior plywood are used.

Figure 1: Exploded View

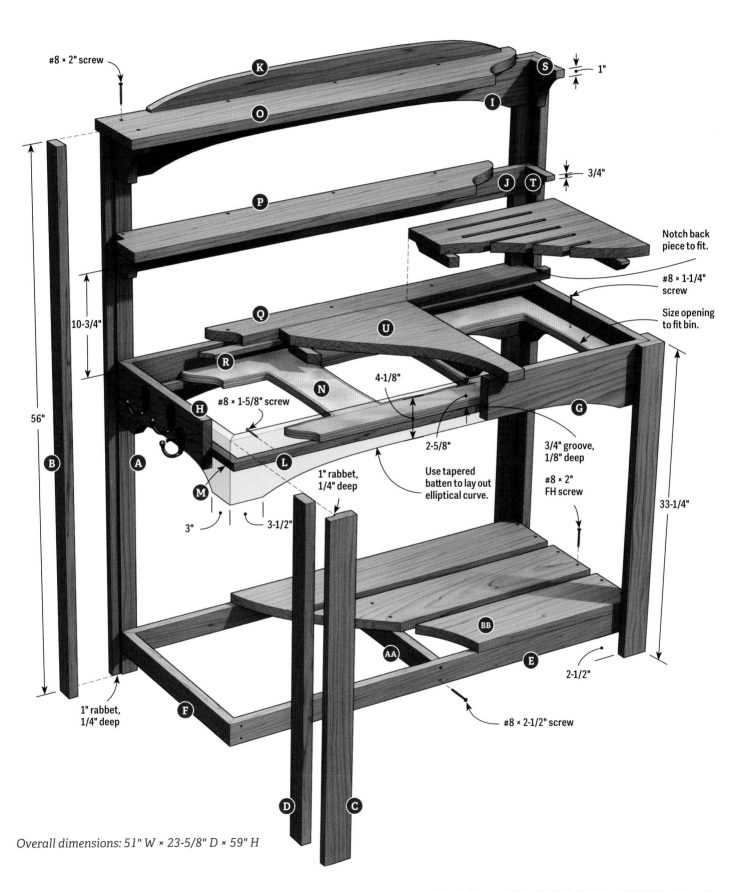

#8 × 2" screw

K

O

I

S

1"

J

T

3/4"

P

Notch back piece to fit.

#8 × 1-1/4" screw

Q

U

Size opening to fit bin.

R

4-1/8"

N

#8 × 1-5/8" screw

H

2-5/8"

G

3/4" groove, 1/8" deep

#8 × 2" FH screw

B

A

L

Use tapered batten to lay out elliptical curve.

33-1/4"

56"

10-3/4"

M

1" rabbet, 1/4" deep

3"

3-1/2"

BB

AA

E

2-1/2"

1" rabbet, 1/4" deep

F

#8 × 2-1/2" screw

D

C

Overall dimensions: 51" W × 23-5/8" D × 59" H

Figure 2: Making
a Tapered Batten

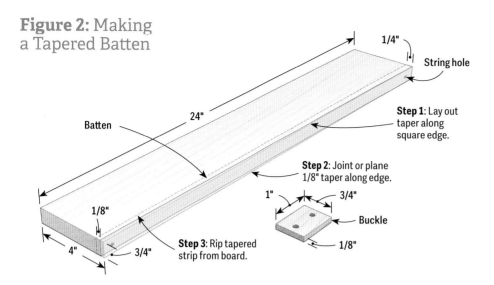

1/4"
String hole

Batten

24"

Step 1: Lay out
taper along
square edge.

Step 2: Joint or plane
1/8" taper along edge.

1/8"

1"   3/4"
Buckle

4"   3/4"
1/8"

Step 3: Rip tapered
strip from board.

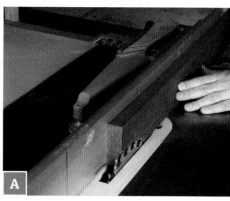

Cut leg rabbets. Use a dado blade to cut a 1/4"-deep rabbet on the inside faces of the wider leg components. The rabbets help with leg assembly.

Make the legs & stretchers

1. Cut the wide **(A, C)** and narrow **(B, D)** pieces for the back and front legs to the sizes shown in the **Cut List**. Install a 1/4" dado set in your table saw, adjust the dado height to match the thickness of your stock, and then rabbet the inside faces of the wide leg pieces **(Photo A)**. This rabbet provides a shoulder that will help align the leg pieces during glue-up.

Apply exterior glue to the rabbet on the wide legs **(A, C)**, and then clamp them to their mating narrow legs **(B, D)** to make four L-shaped leg assemblies **(A/B** and **C/D)**.

2. Cut the front, back, and side stretchers **(E, F)**, the front, back, and side aprons **(G, H)**, and the top and middle shelf supports **(I, J)** to the sizes shown in the **Cut List**.

3. Make a tapered batten and a buckle to lay out the elliptical curves on the aprons and shelf support **(Figure 2)**. Drill holes in the batten and buckle. Thread the buckle

between the ends so that the string can be pulled taut, like a bow.

4. Lay out the curves on the aprons **(G, H)** and the top shelf support **(I)** **(Photo B)**. The curves start 3-1/2" in from either end of the front and back aprons **(G)**, and 3" in on the side aprons **(H)** **(Figure 1)**. The aprons and support are 4-1/8" wide at their center points.

5. Cut the curves on the aprons **(G, H)** and the top shelf support **(I)** with a jigsaw or a bandsaw. Save one of the cutoffs to use for the crest rail **(K)**. Make up a curved sanding block and sand the curves fair, using coarse sandpaper **(Photo C)**. After removing any lumps, finish-sand through 220 grit.

6. Cut 3/4" wide by 1/8" deep grooves on the inside faces in each of the four aprons **(G, H)** for the cleats **(L, M)** that support the bin holder **(N)** **(Figure 1)**. Miter-cut the cleats to the sizes specified in

Mark the curves. Clamp the string to the buckle to keep it taut; then trace the curve along the aprons. Mark the curve's start and end points on the batten.

Sand the curves on the aprons. Use a custom sanding block suited to the curve.

Assemble. After drilling and countersinking screw holes through the stretchers and aprons, screw each part to its leg assembly.

Mark bin locations. Space the bins evenly across the bin holder and trace around them. Cut the openings so that the bins drop in place.

the **Cut List.** Fasten them in their grooves with exterior glue and 1-5/8" screws. Be sure to predrill for the screws to avoid splitting.

Assemble the bench

1 Using a miter saw, miter the ends of the front/back and side stretchers **(E, F)**, front/back and side aprons **(G, H)**, and the top and middle shelf supports **(I, J)** to 45°. Place each stretcher or apron in position against its leg, and drill a pilot hole, clearance hole, and countersink for 1-5/8" screws. Then screw the parts together using exterior glue **(Photo D)**. Next, glue and screw the shelf supports in place **(Figure 1)**.

2. Cut the bin holder **(N)** from exterior plywood to the size listed in the **Cut List.** Next, trace the openings for the three bins **(Photo E)**. Make a second layout line 1/4" inside each of the traced lines. Cut along these inner lines with a jigsaw. Screw the holder to the cleats **(L, M)** with 1-1/4" screws.

NOTE: Almost any wide-lipped container will work. I purchased these four-gallon storage bins at my home center.

Hot Stuff: Thermo-Wood

While cedar, cypress, and redwood make great choices for outdoor projects, I made this bench from thermally treated (or "thermo-") wood. Thermo-wood is heated to temperatures much higher than normal kiln-drying (400° F). In addition to changing the wood's color, the process makes the wood harder, more stable, and resistant to bugs and decay—without any chemicals. In my area, thermo-poplar costs about 30% more than regular poplar. I found it pleasant to work with, although it was dustier and more brittle than normal kiln-dried stock. The color, similar to aged cherry, runs completely through the wood. It will fade if left untreated, but the wood will withstand decades of outdoor use.

Treated poplar

Untreated poplar

Rip the strips. Use the blunt end of a featherboard as a fence-setting stopblock when ripping a series of narrow strips.

Prepare to glue. Tack the spacer slats to the regular slats prior to gluing to prevent the parts from slipping out of alignment under clamp pressure.

3. Cut the top and middle shelves **(O, P)**, the back piece **(Q)**, and the ledger **(R)** to the sizes listed in the **Cut List**. Notch the back corners of the middle shelf and the back piece so they fit inside the legs **(Figure 1)**.

4. Cut the shelf brackets **(S, T)** to the sizes in the **Cut List**. Crosscut one end of each at 45°. On the opposite end, trace a quart-sized can to lay out a decorative curve on the lower corner of each piece. Cut along your layout lines and sand the curves true. (Before cutting the curves, be sure each bracket is a mirror image of its partner, so you end up with the angled cuts on the inside face of each piece.)

5. Drill and countersink the shelf brackets **(S, T)**, and then attach them to the back leg assemblies **(A/B)** with exterior glue and 1-5/8" screws. Drill and countersink the ledger

(R) and fasten it to the underside of the back piece **(Q)** with glue and 1-1/4" screws. Center the ledger from end to end with its front edge extending past the front edge of the back piece by about 5/8". Drill and countersink screw holes for the shelves **(O, P)** and the back piece **(Q)** and attach them with 2" screws.

Make the top panels

1. Cut the solid center panel **(U)** to the size in the **Cut List**. Edge-glue pieces as needed to make up the required width. Also cut the pieces for the front slats **(V)**, regular slats **(W)**, and long and short spacers **(X, Y)** to the sizes listed.

To rip the narrow spacers, position a stopblock in front of the blade to its left **(Photo F)**. Set the stop so that the distance from its end to the blade path equals the width of the spacer. Move the rip fence over until your workpiece touches the

stopblock and make the cut. Readjust the fence for each subsequent cut.

2. To glue up the slotted panels, fasten one long spacer **(X)** and one short spacer **(Y)** to each of the regular slats **(W)** using exterior glue and 3d finish nails **(Photo G)**. Glue six of the spacer/slat assemblies to each of the front slats **(V)**.

3. Cut the battens **(Z)** to the size listed in the **Cut List**. Check their length against your assembled bench: the battens should be about 1/8" shorter than the distance from the front edge of the ledger **(R)** to the inside of the front apron **(G)**. Cut both ends of each batten at 45°, creating a 3/4"-wide chamfer **(Figure 3)**.

4. Drill three 3/16"-diameter holes through each batten **(Z)**, a hole 1-1/4" in from each end, and one in the center. Countersink and counterbore

Figure 3: Top Panel

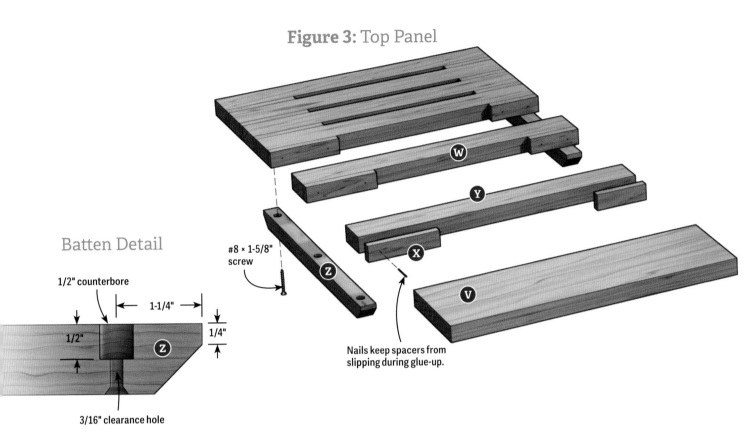

Batten Detail

1/2" counterbore

1-1/4"

1/2"

1/4"

3/16" clearance hole

#8 × 1-5/8" screw

Nails keep spacers from slipping during glue-up.

the holes (batten detail, **Figure 3**). This creates a little space for the screws to move as the panel expands and contracts with changes in humidity.

5. Screw two battens **(Z)** to the underside of each top panel **(Photo H)**. Position the battens 3/8" in from the ends of the solid center panel and 3/8" in from the inside ends of the slotted panels. Position the second batten on each of the slotted panels so it will fall just inside the side apron **(H)**. From front to back, position all the battens so the rear edge of each panel sits on the ledger **(R)** with its back edge butted up to the back piece **(Q)**.

Assemble the panels. Fasten the battens to the undersides of the top panels with 1-5/8" screws. Omit glue to allow the panels to move with changes in humidity.

Finish up

1. Sand the crest rail **(K)** to a smooth curve. Cut its ends to terminate with a 1/4"-wide flat instead of a sharp point. Attach the rail by gluing it to the top shelf **(O)**, and screwing it in place from underneath. Use 2" screws, and be sure to predrill the holes.

2. Cut the center support **(AA)** to the size listed in the **Cut List**. Center it from side to side between the front and back stretchers **(E)**, and screw it in place with 2-1/2" screws.

3. Cut the bottom shelves **(BB)** to the size in the **Cut List**. Screw them to the side stretchers **(F)** and center support **(AA)** with 2" screws.

4. Finish the bench with a clear outdoor finish. Screw the tool hooks in place along the side stretchers and start planting.

Potting Bench Supply & Cut List

	Part	Thickness	Width	Length	Qty.
A	Wide back leg	1"	2-3/4"	56"	2
B	Narrow back leg	1"	2"	56"	2
C	Wide front leg	1"	2-3/4"	33-1/4"	2
D	Narrow front leg	1"	2"	33-1/4"	2
E	Front/back stretcher	1"	2-1/4"	48"	2
F	Side stretcher	1"	2-1/4"	21-5/8"	2
G	Front/back apron	1"	6-1/4"	48"	2
H	Side aprons	1"	6-1/4"	21-5/8"	2
I	Top shelf support	1"	4-1/2"	48"	1
J	Middle shelf support	1"	2-3/4"	48"	1
K	Crest rail	1"	2"	40"	1
L	Front/back cleat	3/4"	7/8"	46-1/4"	2
M	Side cleat	3/4"	7/8"	19-7/8"	2
N	Bin holder	3/4"	19-5/8"	46"	1
O	Top shelf	1"	7-1/4"	51"	1
P	Middle shelf	1"	6"	50"	1
Q	Back piece	1"	3-3/4"	51"	1
R	Ledger	1/2"	1-1/2"	46"	1
S	Top shelf bracket	1"	4-1/2"	5-1/2"	2
T	Middle shelf bracket	1"	2-3/4"	4-3/4"	2
U	Center panel	1"	20-1/2"	15"	1
V	Front slat	1"	5-1/2"	18"	2
W	Regular slat	1"	2"	18"	12
X	Long spacer	1/2"	1"	4-1/2"	12
Y	Short spacer	1/2"	1"	3-1/4"	12
Z	Batten	1"	1"	17"	6
AA	Center support	1"	2-1/4"	19-5/8"	1
BB	Bottom shelf board	1"	6-1/2"	48"	3
	Supplies				
	#8 stainless steel (SS) screws			1-1/4"	
	#8 SS screws			1-5/8"	
	#8 SS screws			2"	
	#8 SS screws			2-1/2"	
	4-gallon storage bins				3
	3d finish nails				
	Robe hooks				3

Garden Arbor

Elegant design and rock-solid joinery make this welcoming structure the envy of the neighborhood.

By Alan Turner

When spring blooms, many woodworkers turn their attention from the shop to the garden. This arbor—plus its matching gate on p. 120—takes dead aim at both passions. Handsome but without excess adornment, this Arts & Crafts–inspired project provides an inviting entrance to a thoughtfully landscaped backyard or patio area. And with any of three complementary fence ideas on p. 127, you can enclose a garden or contain Fido's urge to romp and roam.

As a woodworking project, the arbor will teach you how to use your router with a few simple jigs to cut precise mortises and perfectly shaped curves. Another surprising detail about this project is the shop-friendly subassemblies. Despite its impressive size, this arbor is designed so that you can build the parts when there's still snow on the ground and quickly install it outside as soon as the weather allows.

NOTE: Both the arbor and gate were made from grade "D and better" western red cedar. Cedar is a natural choice for large outdoor structures because it's lightweight, easy to work, and resistant to decay. To find suitable material, you may need to go to a specialty lumberyard. Pressure-treated pine, although less expensive and easier to find, isn't recommended for this project. Treated wood can be brutal on bits and blades.

Start with the arbor sides

1. Begin this project by making the mortising templates explained in "Shop-Made Mortising Jigs" on p. 113.

2. Crosscut the posts **(A)** and stretchers **(D)** to length plus 4". (Add the below-frost length if sinking the posts to provide better support for the gate. See the **Cut List** for dimensions and the sidebar below.) Now, thickness-plane these parts to square off the rounded corners. Working in 1/16"-deep increments, plane one post face, rotate the post 90°, and plane the adjacent edge. Plane all four post and two stretcher faces before lowering the cutting head. After removing the roundovers, the finished dimension should be 3-1/4" square.

TIP: Look for stock that's free of any pith (center of the tree), especially when picking corner posts. Pithy posts tend to twist over time.

3. Crosscut the freshly squared posts **(A)** to 83-1/2". Include the frost depth if appropriate.

4. Starting at 83-1/2" down from the top end of posts **(A)**, mark the mortise locations **(Figure 1)**. Next, clamp all four posts side-by-side **(Photo A)**. Make sure that the ends are flush before transferring the mortise locations onto the remaining three posts.

5. Mortise the posts **(A)** using the lower rung and upper rung templates (p. 113). Begin by aligning the appropriate template with your mortise marks and clamping it in place. Chuck a 7/8" spade bit into a drill and remove the bulk of the waste **(Photo B)**.

TIP: Make your mortises 1/8" deeper than the length of your tenons. The extra space gives excess glue a place to go—instead of oozing out the sides—when you insert the tenons.

6. Next, chuck an upcut spiral bit into your hand-held router. Position the tool on the jig, turn it on, and plunge the mortising bit to full depth at the corners of the mortise; then raise the bit and rout from side to side in 1/4"-deep increments to clean up the mortise walls and bottom **(Photo C)**. After routing the four mortises for the lower rungs, use the upper rung template to rout the remaining 16 mortises.

TIP: Filing a small notch in the top and bottom of the jigs' mortise openings will make the layout lines visible without affecting the accuracy of your jigs.

7. Referring to the **Cutting Diagram**, rip enough 2x6 stock to make eight 19" long upper rungs **(B)** and two lower rungs **(C)**. Saw off the rounded corners before ripping the rungs to final **Cut List** width. (Cut an extra upper and lower rung to fine-tune the tenon-cutting setups.)

8. Crosscut rungs **(B, C)** to their final length by clamping a stopblock to

Batch-mark. Marking out all the mortises at once is faster than using a tape and eliminates the errors that can sneak in when making repetitive measurements.

Remove the waste. Mark the mortise depth on the bit's shank to avoid drilling too deeply.

Match the Post Length to Your Needs

The length of the post **(A)** given in the **Cut List** assumes that you're using a metal post base or post stake for post-footing options **(Figure 7)**. If attaching the gate, setting the posts in concrete offers the most stable and permanent option. If you choose this method, buy posts that are long enough to be positioned below the frost line.

Figure 1: Exploded View

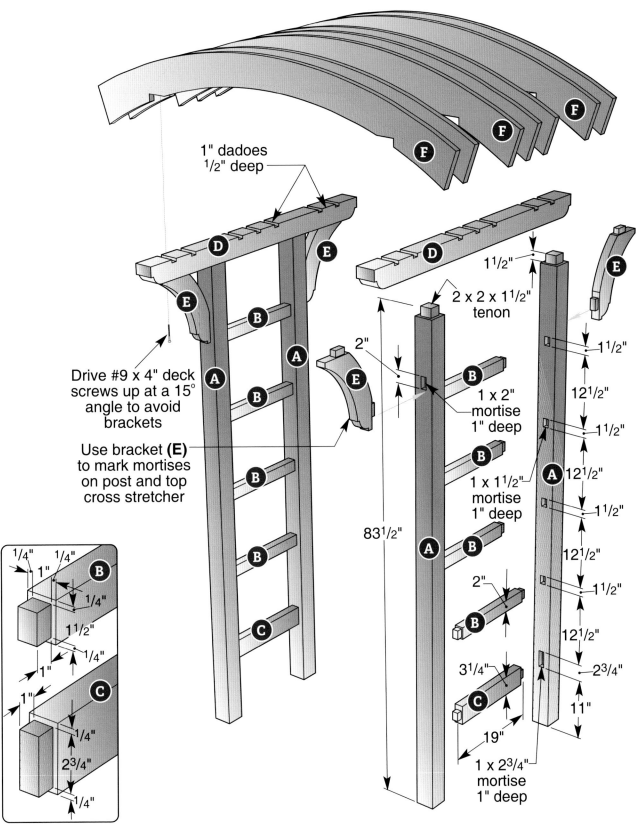

1" dadoes
1/2" deep

Drive #9 x 4" deck screws up at a 15° angle to avoid brackets

Use bracket **(E)** to mark mortises on post and top cross stretcher

83 1/2"

2 x 2 x 1 1/2" tenon

1 1/2"

2"

1 x 2" mortise 1" deep

1 x 1 1/2" mortise 1" deep

2"

3 1/4"

19"

1 x 2 3/4" mortise 1" deep

1 1/2"

12 1/2"

1 1/2"

12 1/2"

1 1/2"

12 1/2"

1 1/2"

12 1/2"

2 3/4"

11"

1/4"   1/4"
1"
1/4"
1 1/2"
1/4"
1"
1"
1/4"
2 3/4"
1/4"

Overall dimensions: 51" D × 71" W × 93-1/4" H

your miter saw and making a test cut. Adjust as needed and make your cuts.

9. Cut the upper **(B)** and lower rung **(C)** tenon shoulders on the table saw by first drawing a line 1" in from the end of a test rung. Next, raise the blade height to 1/4" and adjust the rip fence so the pencil line remains after

C

Clean up the walls and bottom. The jig keeps the router from cutting outside the lines. Vacuum out the cavity and inspect your work before unclamping the jig.

D

Cut rung tenon shoulders. Butt the ends to each rung against the fence to ensure even tenon shoulders. Use a miter gauge to guide the rungs over the saw blade.

E

Saw cheeks. Bandsaw the cheeks so the waste falls away from the fence. Use a stopblock to control the length of cut.

you cut. Then, using your miter gauge, test-cut a tenon and check your work. The shoulder-to-end dimension should be exactly 1". Now, cut the shoulders on all of the upper rungs **(B)** and the lower rungs **(C) (Photo D)**.

10. Cut the rung cheeks on the bandsaw by starting with your test rung. Adjust the bandsaw's fence and attach a stopblock on it so that the blade cuts the cheek and the waste falls to the outside **(Photo E)**. Finally, round the edges of the tenons with a file so that they'll slide smoothly into the mortises.

11. Cut tenons on the ends of the posts **(A)**. The length of the posts makes them too awkward to maneuver on the table saw; clamp all four posts together side-by-side with the ends flush. Mark your tenon locations and use a circular saw and straightedge to make the 5/8" deep cut **(Photo F)**. Turn the posts 90° and repeat the cut. Do all four post sides this way. Cut the cheeks as in Step 10.

12. Crosscut the top cross stretchers **(D)** to 51". Make a pattern for the stretcher ends from 1/4"-thick hardboard **(Figure 2)**. Trace the end pattern on both sides of each end. Next, cut out the curve using either a bandsaw or a jigsaw with a 6"-long blade. Finally, clean up your cut with rasps, files, and sandpaper. Work from the outside edges toward the center to avoid chipping on the back edges.

13. Mark (don't measure) the post mortises. The locations of the post mortises in the top cross stretcher **(D)** depend on the side assemblies. For the best fit, dry-assemble each side assembly and pull it tightly together with clamps. Center a top cross stretcher **(D)** between the two posts **(A)** and transfer the locations of the posts' tenons onto the bottom face of the top cross stretcher **(D)**. Repeat the assembly and marking process with the opposite side. Label each stretcher/side pair so that they will be matched together later.

TIP: Use the post-mortising jigs to check the fit of the rungs before sticking them into the posts.

14. Rout the mortises in the top cross stretcher **(D)** using the post-mortising jigs.

Make the corner brackets

1. Make an enlarged copy of the corner bracket pattern **(Figure 8)**. Adhere the pattern onto a 5-1/4"-wide piece of 1/4"-thick hardboard, then bandsaw and sand it to shape.

2. From 2 × 6 stock, cut two corner bracket blanks for the brackets **(E)** to 18" long. Joint one edge of each piece to remove the roundovers and, using your miter saw, cut one end of each blank at 35°.

TIP: When making curved parts, cut the joinery before cutting the curves. A straightedge provides a reliable reference for both marking and cutting.

Shop-Made Mortising Jigs

To make the jigs, we used four 10" × 11" pieces of 1/4"-thick hardboard, a combination square, glue, and finishing nails or 3/4"-long screws. When in use, the scrapwood cleats guide the router while the fence and clamps hold the jig in place on your work. The arbor requires four router mortising jigs: lower rung, upper rung, post, and corner bracket. Build as shown and label each template to avoid confusion. Determine your router's offset and mark that distance outside of your mortise lines. (The offset is the distance between the outside edge of your router's base and the outside edge of your installed upcut spiral bit.) To do this, position the router so that the bit touches each inside corner of your mortise opening and draw a box around the penciled arcs to reveal the offset distance.

Next, attach the cleats to the base along the outside edges of the penciled box with glue and screws or finish nails. (As shown at right, open corners enable chips to fall free instead of clogging the jig.)

Finally, lay out a mock mortise on a piece of test scrap that matches the workpiece. Clamp the jig to the scrap and check that the mortise aligns with your layout lines. Make a test cut, following the instructions in Step 5 and 6 on p. 110.

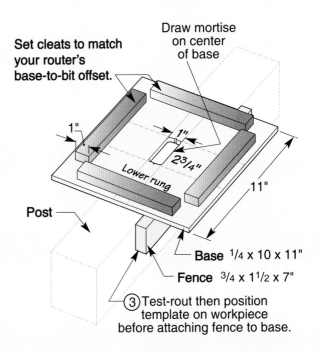

Set cleats to match your router's base-to-bit offset.

Draw mortise on center of base

1"

1"

2³/₄"

Lower rung

11"

Post

Base 1/4 x 10 x 11"

Fence 3/4 x 1¹/2 x 7"

③ Test-rout then position template on workpiece before attaching fence to base.

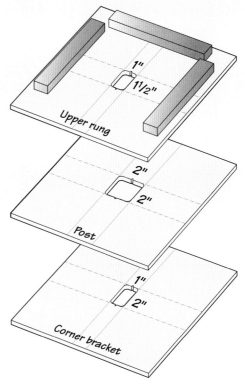

1"

1¹/₂"

Upper rung

2"

2"

Post

1"

2"

Corner bracket

Cut post tenon shoulders. Insert a spacer between the fence and your workpiece to cut the even tenon shoulders. Use a stopblock to set the tenon length.

3. Next, place the corner bracket pattern **(Figure 8)** on the bracket blanks **(E)**, aligning the top tenon with the 35° line. Trace the bracket pattern onto both faces of each blank.

4. Make a stop for cutting the bottom tenon angle on the bracket **(E)** blanks on a miter saw. Add a toggle clamp hold-down for securing the bracket blank during the cutting operation. Position the workpiece, clamp the brace to the miter saw fence, lower the hold-down, and make the cut **(Photo G)**.

5. To cut the corner bracket **(E)** tenon cheeks, install a 5/8" dado cutter set into your table saw and a sacrificial fence on your saw's fence. Set the cutter height to 1/4", and set the sacrificial fence 1" from the outside edge of the dado set. Now cut both ends of each corner bracket **(E)** to establish the tenon shoulders **(Photo H)**. Reset the fence, burying the blade in a sacrificial fence, to complete the ends of the tenon cheeks.

6. Locate, mark, and cut the bracket tenons to 2" wide **(Photo I)**. Now make the shoulder cuts, cutting to the line. Clean up the cuts with a chisel.

7. Bandsaw or jigsaw the curves on the corner brackets **(E)**. Cut as close to the line as possible, and smooth with rasps and files or a spindle sander.

8. Assemble both side assemblies to locate the corner bracket **(E)** mortises. Using the corner brackets, transfer the bracket mortise locations to the posts **(A)** and top cross stretchers **(D)**. Disassemble the side assemblies and rout the mortises using the corner bracket mortising jig (p. 113). After you've cut all eight mortises, reassemble the sides and test-fit the corner brackets. Label each bracket for later assembly.

Make the bonnet ribs

NOTE: There are seven identical bonnet ribs (F). If drawn inside a rectangle, each would be approximately 14-3/4" wide by 71" long. Here you'll see how to create a wider board from a 2 × 12 by reattaching cutoffs onto the bottom of your stock.

1. Make the template for the flared bonnet ribs **(F)** by attaching a 16" × 72" piece of 1/4"-thick hardboard to your floor with double-faced tape. Follow the three-step layout sequence **(Figure 3)**. (A pair of trammel points will help, but you can get by with a 2"-wide strip of plywood, pencil, and finish nails.) After laying out the top and bottom curves, measure and mark the ends of the bonnet rib pattern and the notches **(Figure 4)**. Cut out the template on your bandsaw, then carefully sand up to your layout lines to create a smooth, or fair, curve.

2. Thickness 2 × 12 stock to 1" for the 1 × 12 bonnet ribs **(F)** and edge-joint one edge. Position the bonnet rib template on top of your rib stock **(Figure 5)** so that the jointed edge runs along the bottom of the rib. (At this point, the template is still wider than your stock.) Using a bandsaw or jigsaw, cut the bottom curve about 1/8" to the waste side of your line.

TIP: To shape the gently curved rib pattern, glue 60-grit paper to

Figure 2: Stretcher Part View

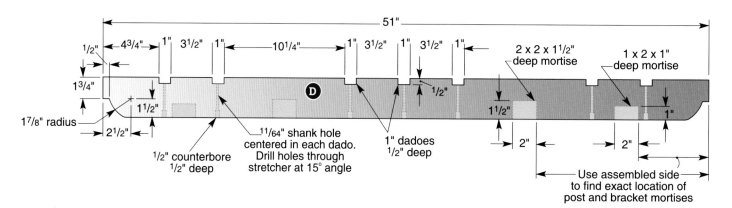

a 2" wide by 11" long piece of 1/8" plywood using a quick-release contact cement, to make a flexible "file."

3. Make two rectangles from the jointed bottom cutoffs and epoxy them to the bottom corners of all seven rib blanks **(Figure 5)**.

4. Give the ribs about 24 hours to fully cure; then remove the clamps and trace the rib pattern on your board. Cut the ends to finished length using a miter saw set at 20°. Cut the top arc and the remaining portions of the bottom arc about 1/8" outside of your pencil lines.

5. Rout half of the bonnet ribs **(F)**. To avoid tear out, always rout downhill to the grain. To succeed, you'll need two bearing-guided router bits: a pattern routing bit with a top bearing and a flush-trim bit with a bottom-mounted bearing. Begin the process by sticking the pattern on top of the rib blank and orienting the blank so that the bottom ends are pointing toward you. Now, with your router and a pattern-routing bit, guide the bearing against the left-hand half of the arch bottom; then reposition the router and shape the right-hand half of the top. Try to start and stop your cuts at or near the rib's centerpoint so that the bit's rotation doesn't lift or tear out opposing grain.

TIP: Fresh epoxy squeeze-out can be cleaned up with acetone or lacquer thinner. If you miss a spot, watch and wait for it to get to the green

stage. This partially cured point is the perfect time to remove excess with a block plane because it's not sticky but is softer than when fully cured.

6. Finish routing the rest of the rib with a flush-trim bit. Flip the rib **(F)** so that pattern sits under your stock. Chuck a bottom-bearing flush-trim bit into your router and trim the remaining two edges.

7. Using the pattern, mark and then bandsaw or jigsaw the notch in the ribs **(F)**.

8. Dado the top cross stretcher **(D)** to fit the bonnet ribs **(F)** by first placing two stretchers side-by-side. Mark the location of the dadoes for both bonnet ribs at the same time with a square and pencil **(Figure 2)**. Use a bonnet rib **(F)** to check that the dadoes are wide enough. Then use your table saw and dado cutter set, or router and straightedge guide, to cut the 1/2"-deep dadoes.

TIP: Ball bearing–guided spiral bits are expensive, but the shearing cut can prevent tear out, even when cutting against the grain.

Assemble the arbor sides

The glue-up proceeds in two stages. The first creates the "ladder" assembly; the second adds the corner brackets **(E)** and top cross stretcher **(D)**. Choose an epoxy with a long open time so you can make adjustments and arrange your clamps where needed.

Cut the bottom tenon. With the miter saw set for a 35° cut, clamp a brace to the fence, secure the workpiece to it, and angle-cut the end of the bottom tenon on the bracket blank at 55°.

Cut bracket angled tenons. Press the ends of the corner brackets against the fence to cut the angled tenons. The resulting tenon should be 1" thick.

Handsaw the bracket tenons. Mark the width of the bracket tenons; then cut them to finished dimensions with a bandsaw or dovetail saw.

1. Clean up your parts before glue-up. To lift dents, place a damp cloth over spot, then lightly run a hot iron over it. Lightly sand to 120 grit.

2. Next, glue the upper and lower rungs to the posts, placing the top cross stretcher **(D)** on the post tenons without glue to help maintain the squareness of the assembly. Center clamps across each rung and let the epoxy cure overnight.

3. Insert the corner brackets **(E)** in the posts **(A)**, then clamp the top cross stretcher **(D)** in position **(Photo J)**. Repeat the process for the remaining side.

TIP: *A thin coat of epoxy on the end grain of a joint will seal the wood and prevent or reduce wicking, preserving the joint for a long period of time. Similarly coating the bottom of the posts is also recommended.*

---

4. Assemble the arbor in your shop. Stand the two sides on the floor. To keep the sides from tipping, clamp a pair of 42"-long 2 × 4 spacers between the sides. Insert the bonnet ribs into the dados.

Figure 3: Making the Rib Template

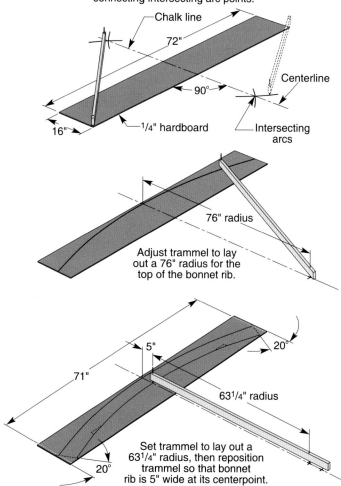

To establish a perpendicular line through the middle of your template, swing trammel from opposite corners. Snap a line connecting intersecting arc points.

Figure 4: Rib Part View

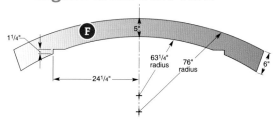

Figure 5: Bonnet Rib Process

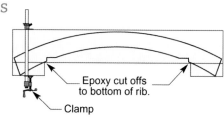

5. Screw the top cross stretcher **(D)** to the bonnet ribs **(F)**. To do this, drill a 1-3/64" hole at a 15° angle up through the bottom of each stretcher **(D) (Figure 1)**. Aim for the center of each rib **(F)** about 3/4" in from the inside edge. After drilling the pilot hole, use a 3/8" twist drill to create a 1/2"-deep counterbore in the stretcher **(D)**. This allows the screw to be countersunk well out of sight. Drill a 1/8" pilot hole about 2" into the bottom of each bonnet rib **(F)**. Mark the ribs before disassembly so that they can be matched to their dadoes.

6. Finish your arbor. Stain or paint the arbor after final assembly and drilling, but before installation. A good defense is a gray oil-based exterior primer, followed by an acrylic deck paint.

Set in the footings & install the arbor

NOTE: Digging even a small misplaced hole can disrupt service to an entire neighborhood, or kill you. An easy—and free—way to avoid such risks is by calling 811. This call will connect you with a professional utility locator who will mark out nearby utility lines so that you know where it's safe to locate your arbor.

1. If you want your arbor to last, make sure you set it on solid footing. Screw together a jig from scrap lumber and leftover post stock, matching the dimensions of your arbor **(Figure 6)**. Use the frame to level the tops **(Photo K)**.

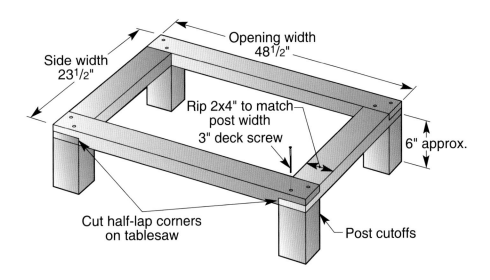

Figure 6: Footing Placement Frame

Opening width 48¹/₂"

Side width 23¹/₂"

Rip 2x4" to match post width

3" deck screw

6" approx.

Cut half-lap corners on tablesaw

Post cutoffs

2. Set the arbor sides in the post stakes **(Photo L)**. You'll need to insert shims into the post stakes or standoffs to account for the wood you removed when squaring the posts **(A)**. If you're not planning to build the gate, metal post stakes are a quick and easy way to set the posts **(Figure 7)**. A concrete footing would offer more support to the arbor frame, and is recommended if you intend to include a gate and/or fence.

3. Set the bonnet ribs **(F)** into the top cross stretchers **(D) (Photo M)**. To avoid chuck damage to the corner brackets, use 6" long drill bits. Drive a 4"-long #9 deck screw through the stretcher and into the bonnet ribs to pull the arbor together.

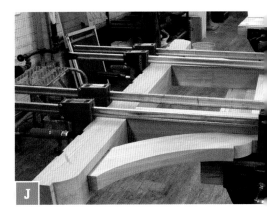

Clamp the assembly. Position the clamps perpendicular to the top cross to prevent bending the ends or warping the assembly.

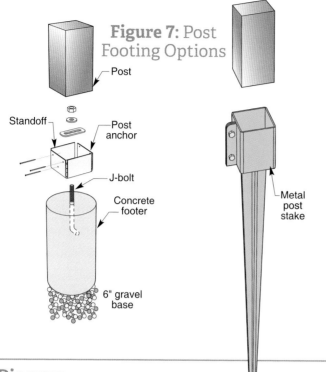

Figure 7: Post Footing Options

Post

Standoff

Post anchor

J-bolt

Concrete footer

6" gravel base

Metal post stake

K

Position the arbor. Use a scrapwood positioning jig to mark the exact locations for the bolt-down standoffs or to adjust the height of the post stakes.

Cutting Diagram

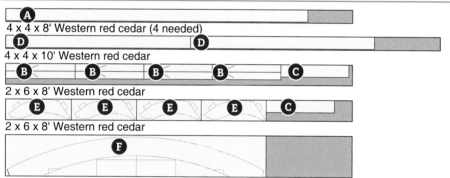

A
4 x 4 x 8' Western red cedar (4 needed)

D **D**
4 x 4 x 10' Western red cedar

B **B** **B** **B** **C**
2 x 6 x 8' Western red cedar

E **E** **E** **E** **C**
2 x 6 x 8' Western red cedar

F
2 x 12 x 8' Western red cedar (7 needed)

L

Tip the arbor sides in place. Use a helper or attach a scrapwood brace before attaching the bonnet ribs.

Garden Arbor Supply & Cut List

	Part	Thickness	Width	Length	Qty.
A	Post	3-1/4"	3-1/4"	83-1/2"	4
B	Upper rung	1-1/2"	2"	19"	8
C	Lower rung	1-1/2"	3-1/4"	19"	2
D	Top cross stretcher	3-1/4"	3-1/4"	51"	2
E*	Bracket	1-1/2	5-1/4"	16-7/8"	4
F*	Bonnet rib	1"	14-5/8"	71"	7
	Supplies				
	#9 deck screws			4"	

Indicates that parts are initially cut oversized. See instructions.

M

Set the bonnet ribs. Carefully place them in the dadoes to keep touch-up painting to a minimum. Screw them in place.

Figure 8: Corner Template

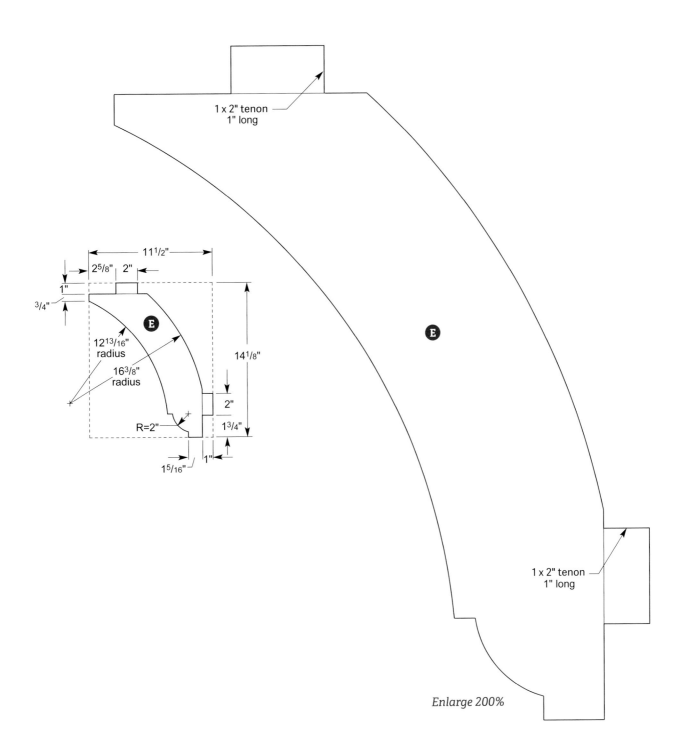

1 x 2" tenon
1" long

11¹/₂"

2⁵/₈"   2"

1"

³/₄"

12¹³/₁₆"
radius

16³/₈"
radius

E

R=2"

14¹/₈"

2"

1³/₄"

1⁵/₁₆"   1"

E

1 x 2" tenon
1" long

Enlarge 200%

Arbor Gate

Keep the world at bay with an elegant companion to a graceful arbor.

By Alan Turner

This curved-top gate is the perfect complement to your new arbor. As you can see, the top rail, the ends of the stiles, and even the custom-made iron hinges were arched to match the arbor's ribbed bonnet. Like the arbor, the gate is built to last from western red cedar. The rails attach to the stiles using solid mortise-and-tenon joinery. Matching the curve of the top rail to the top of the center stile might appear daunting, but here you'll learn how to make a template and use your router for a seamless fit.

Begin with the gate frame

1. Referring to the **Cut List**, crosscut the stiles **(A)**, bottom rail **(B)**, and center stile **(D)** to length plus a few inches from 2 × 6 stock **(Figure 1)**. Make the top rail **(C)** from 2 × 10 stock. Surface-plane all five pieces to 1-3/8" thick. Using your table saw, rip a square edge on all pieces, then rip the stiles **(A)**, bottom rail **(B)**, and center stile **(D)** to 4-1/4" wide. The top rail **(C)** will be sawn to width later.

2. Cut the frame to fit the arbor. Referring to the **Cut List**, crosscut the stiles **(A)** and center stile **(D)** to final length. The center stile **(D)** is left long. It will be trimmed to fit later during assembly. See the note below before cutting the bottom rail **(B)** and top rail **(C)** to final length.

NOTE: Measure the width of your arbor opening before cutting the rails to final length. This gate is designed with 7/8" of clearance on the hinge side and an equal 7/8" gap on the latch side, for a post-to-post distance of 42". You may need to adjust the length of the rails to fit your arbor.

3. Make a template for the top rail **(C)** by first chucking a 1/2"-diameter straight bit into your handheld router. Then attach the router's base to a 54"-long strip of plywood. Plunge the bit through the plywood base. Measure 46-3/4" from the inside edge of the bit and

Figure 1: Exploded View

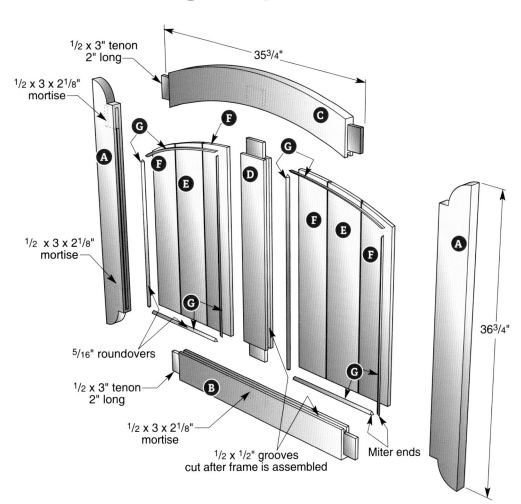

1/2 x 3" tenon 2" long

35³/4"

1/2 x 3 x 2¹/8" mortise

1/2 x 3 x 2¹/8" mortise

⁵/16" roundovers

1/2 x 3" tenon 2" long

1/2 x 3 x 2¹/8" mortise

1/2 x 1/2" grooves cut after frame is assembled

Miter ends

36³/4"

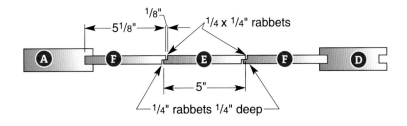

1/8"

5¹/8"

1/4 x 1/4" rabbets

5"

1/4" rabbets 1/4" deep

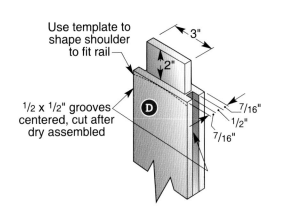

Use template to shape shoulder to fit rail

3"

2"

1/2 x 1/2" grooves centered, cut after dry assembled

7/16"

1/2"

7/16"

drill a 1/8"-diameter pilot hole through the plywood. Cut an 8" × 36" piece of 1/2"-thick MDF or 1/4" hardboard and place it under your router. Now drive a screw through the pilot hole so that it serves as a pivot point. Proceed to rout the top arch **(Photo A.)** Drill a 1/8"-diameter hole 42-1/4" away from the outside edge of your bit on the plywood base. Reposition your jig so that you're using the new hole as your pivot point and rout the bottom arch.

4. Mortise the stiles **(A)** for the tenons on the bottom rail **(B)** and top rail **(C)** where shown using a hollow-chisel mortiser **(Figures 2, 3)**. Add 1/8" to the depths to allow for glue. If you don't own a mortiser, use your drill press and a 1/2"-diameter Forstner bit. Pare the opening with a chisel, establishing clean, square corners.

5. Mortise the bottom rail **(B)** for the center stile **(D)** (refer to dimensions in **Figure 2**).

6. Spray-adhere a copy of the pattern for the stiles **(Figure 6)** onto 1/4"-thick hardboard and cut it out. Now trace the pattern onto both faces of each stile end. Use your table saw to cut the horizontal notches, then bandsaw or jigsaw the curves. Use a rasp and file to erase saw marks and work up to your line. When filing, work from the outer edges to the center to prevent chip-out.

7. Saw the tenons on bottom rail **(B)**, top rail **(C)**, and center stile **(D)** by first cutting the shoulders on the faces of the three pieces with a table saw. Raise the blade to 7/16", adjust the fence to 2" from the outside blade teeth, and cut the shoulders, using your

Figure 2: Parts View

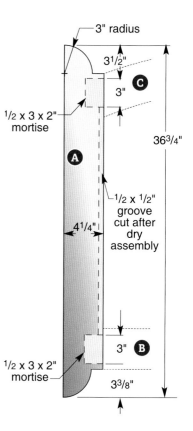

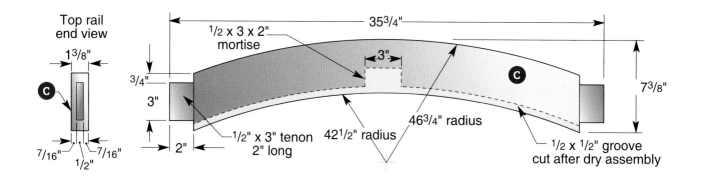

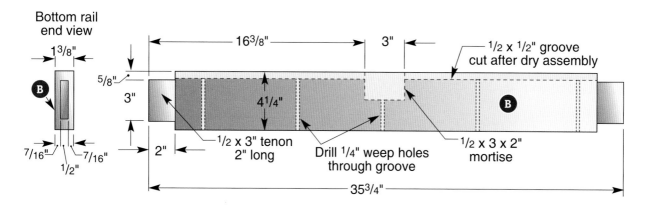

miter gauge. Raise the blade to 5/8" and make the connecting shoulder cuts through the edges of the bottom rail **(B)**, stile **(D)**, and in the bottom edge of rail **(C)**. Raise the saw blade to 2", and, using a tenoning jig, make the cheek cuts on all three pieces **(Photo B)**. Finish cutting the edge shoulders with a bandsaw or handsaw.

8. Use the top rail template to mark the curves on the top rail **(C)**. Cut the bottom curve about 1/4" away from your pencil line. Before sawing the top curve, make the mortise for the center stile **(D)**. Measuring against the pencil line, set your mortiser for a 2-1/8"-deep cut and cut the 1/2" × 3" mortise **(Figure 2)**.

9. Rough-cut the curved top edge of the top rail **(C)** using a bandsaw or jigsaw; then attach the rail pattern **(Figure 6)** to the bottom face of the stock with double-faced tape. With a handheld router and flush-trim bit, pattern-rout the "downhill" grain parts of the curve. Then, chuck a pattern-routing bit into your router, flip the work over so the pattern is on the top, and finish the curve.

Make the center stile & panels to fit the frame

1. Make a curved shoulder template for the center stile **(D)**. Assemble the gate without the center stile **(D)**. Center a 4-1/4"-wide strip of 1/2"-thick MDF under the top rail **(C)** and then trace the bottom curve onto the MDF. Cut to the line, smooth the

curve, and then test the template to make sure that it fits tightly against the bottom of the top rail **(C)**.

2. Shape the center stile **(D)** to fit the top rail **(C)**. To do this, use a combination square and make a pencil line across both faces of the center stile **(D)**, 1/4" below the square-cut tenon shoulder. Clamp the template to the rail so that its top edge touches the line. Using your router and a pattern bit, adjust the bit height so that the cutter grazes the tenon's cheek and routs the curved shoulder **(Photo C)**. Remount the pattern on the opposite side and rout the other shoulder. After routing, trim the top tenon so that it's 2" long from the centerpoint of the curved shoulder to the end.

Cut the curves. Mounting a router to your trammel is an easy way to cleanly cut the curves for the top rail template.

Cut tenon cheeks. Use a table saw and tenoning jig to easily cut the wide tenon cheeks on the rails and stile.

Figure 3: Drawing the Panel Arch

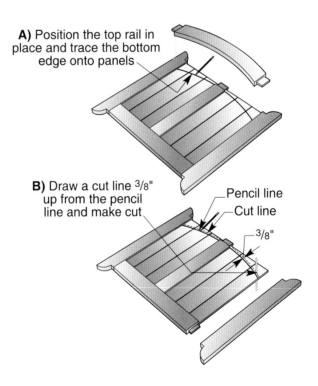

A) Position the top rail in place and trace the bottom edge onto panels

B) Draw a cut line 3/8" up from the pencil line and make cut

Pencil line
Cut line
3/8"

3. Trim the bottom of the center stile **(D)** to fit the gate. Begin by dry-assembling the gate, without the center stile **(D)**, and mark the new shoulder location on the bottom of the center stile with a knife. Recut the bottom rail shoulders on the table saw to the marked length and clean up the cheeks with a chisel. Trim the tenon to fit.

4. Groove the gate frame for the panels. First, dry-assemble and clamp the gate with the center stile. Using your handheld router, install a 1/4" slot cutter, then adjust the bit so that when routing from both sides of the gate you produce a 1/2"-wide centered groove. After routing the framed openings from both sides, disassemble the gate and use a chisel to square

off the rounded corners that the bit couldn't reach. Finally, drill a series of 1/4"-diameter weep holes through the slot on the bottom rail **(B)** where for water drainage **(Figure 2)**.

5. Surface-plane enough 1×6 stock to 1/2" thick to make the inner **(E)** and outer **(F)** panels. (See the **Cutting Diagram**.) Rip the panels to the widths indicated in the **Cut List**. Using your table saw and dado cutter (or router table and straight bit) cut the 1/4" × 1/4" rabbets **(Figure 1)**.

6. Cut the panels to match the curved top by assembling the gate frame, minus the top rail **(C)**. Insert the panels **(E, F)** into the grooves **(Figure 1)**. Next, position the top rail **(C) (Figure 3)**. Make a light pencil

line along the bottom edge of the top rail. Mark 3/8" up from that previous line and, aligning the top with these marks, scribe a second line parallel to the first. Now remove the rail template and bandsaw or jigsaw along this outside line, allowing the panels to fit the frame.

TIP: Save the leftover epoxy. Once it is cured, you'll know that the applied portion is also properly cured.

7. Clamp the bottom rail **(B)** to the bench. Then insert the center stile **(D)** and panel pieces **(Photo D)**. (Some 7/16"-thick strips of scrap can help support the free ends of the panel.) Slide the top rail **(C)** onto the inner panels **(E)**, outer panels **(F)**, and center stile **(D)**.

Figure 4: Gate Hardware Assembly

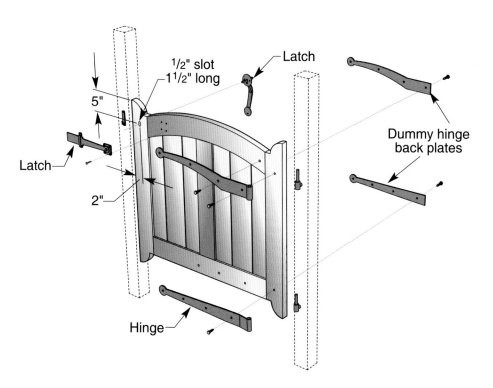

Figure 5: Drilling Pintle Holes

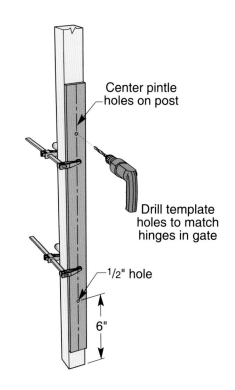

8. Mill the panel beading **(G)** by making the radiused edge first. For safety, the beading pieces are routed, then ripped, from leftover 2× stock. To do this, install a 1/4"-radius roundover bit into your router table and rout each corner. Next, take the board to your table saw. Set the blade height to 5/16", the fence to 5/16", and free each corner in two cuts using a sacrificial push pad. Joint the edge and repeat the routing and sawing process to make additional beading. Miter the bottom corners and cope the top corners to fit the beading to the frame. Attach the beading to the rail and stile edges using pin nails and waterproof glue. Clamp the beading in place to ensure that it doesn't pull away from the nails **(Photo E)**.

9. Sand the gate to 180 grit in preparation for painting. A gray oil-based exterior primer, followed by an acrylic deck paint, is a good defense against the outdoors.

Cutting Diagram

(A)   (A)   (G)
2 x 6 x 8' Western red cedar

(B)   (D)   (G)
2 x 6 x 8' Western red cedar

(C)
2 x 10 x 4' Western red cedar

(E)   (E)   (E)
1 x 6 x 8' Western red cedar

(E)   (F)   (F)
1 x 6 x 8' Western red cedar

Install the hinges & hang the gate

1. To install the strap hinges on the bottom rail **(B)** and top rail **(C)**, strike a centerline for the bolt holes (the hinge does not have parallel sides), then drill and mount **(Figure 4)**. A dummy hinge plate on the gate's back face gives a similar appearance from both sides and works like a giant washer, enabling you to tighten the hinge bolts to the gate.

2. Install the thumb latch by measuring 1-3/4" in from the edge of the door (opposite the hinges) with a combination square and striking a 1" line from 4-1/2" to 5-1/2" down from the top outside end of center stile **(D)**. Strike a parallel line 2-1/4" in from the edge. With 2" in as your center, mortise through the door with a 1/2" drill bit, creating a 1"-long slot for the latch lift. Clean the mortise with a chisel and install the latch door hardware.

Shape the shoulder. Use a shallow-cutting pattern bit to shape the top shoulder of the center stile to fit the top rail.

Assemble the gate. Start from the bottom up. Use spacer blocks to support the free ends of the panel.

Apply the bead. Flex the bead along the top curve to fit it in place. Use clamps and nails to hold it to the top rail until the glue dries.

Arbor Gate Supply & Cut List

Part		Thickness	Width	Length	Qty.
A*	Stile	1-3/8"	4-1/4"	36-3/4"	2
B*	Bottom rail	1-3/8"	4-1/4"	35-3/4"	1
C	Top rail	1-3/8"	7-3/8"	35-3/4"	1
D*	Center stile	1-3/8"	4-1/4"	30"	1
E*	Panel (inner)	1/2"	5"	26"	2
F*	Panel (outer)	1/2"	5-1/8"	26"	4
G*	Beading	5/16"	5/16"	16" (top/bottom), 26" (sides)	4 ea.

Supplies

Arch-top pintle hinges

Dummy hinge back plate pair

Thumb latch

Indicates that parts are initially cut oversized. See instructions.

3. To install the pintles, measure the distance from the bottom of the top hinge to the bottom of the bottom hinge and then make a post boring template from scrap **(Figure 5)**. Drill two 1/2" holes at this exact distance. On site, after the arbor installation, clamp the guide block to the arbor **(Photo F)**. Drill the holes and turn them in. Hang the gate on the pintles.

4. Hang the gate and attach the keeper. The keeper is the last step in the assembly process. Instead of measuring, close the installed gate and transfer the location of the catch onto the post to accurately position the keeper when the gate is shut. Now, fasten the keeper to the post.

Hang the gate. Make a boring jig, drill the holes in the arbor post, and install the threaded pintles by screwing them in place.

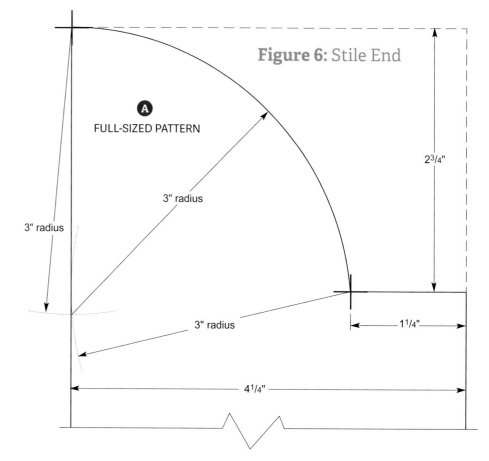

Figure 6: Stile End

Ⓐ FULL-SIZED PATTERN

3" radius

3" radius

3" radius

2³⁄₄"

1¹⁄₄"

4¹⁄₄"

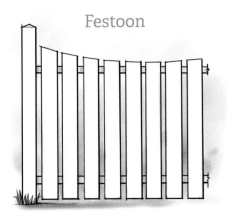

Festoon

Traditional

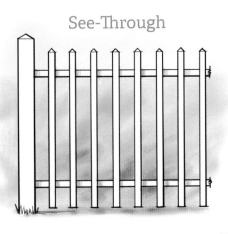

See-Through

A Trio of Fence Ideas

While the arbor and gate make a grand entrance into an attractively landscaped yard, you might want to enclose the area with a complementary fence. Here are three fence ideas to help you do just that. Consider making the 8' long fence sections, attaching picket assemblies to 4 × 4 posts, and maintaining a height equal to or just above the gate's height. Sink the posts to below frost line for maximum durability.

Garden Obelisk

Give your climbing plants the space to soar.

By Tim Snyder

M y wife is an avid gardener, and I love woodworking. We've been able to create some nice projects by combining these two passions, including the garden obelisk featured here. These wooden steeples can be attractive punctuation marks in many yards and gardens, creating focal points that integrate architecture with the natural beauty of climbing plants.

We found that the wooden obelisks we purchased were too easily damaged; their nailed-together joints can't stand up to New England's blustery weather. Why not make a "woodworker's obelisk" that can provide any yard with a peak experience, while standing strong?

If you like this design, I suggest buying enough lumber for two or more. Even if you only use one in your garden, any friend with a green thumb is sure to want one.

Posts, rungs & decorative peak

I ripped all my post and rung stock from cedar 2×6 decking boards, then planed this material 1-3/8" square before cutting parts to finished length. Cypress and pressure-treated pine are also good outdoor wood choices. Whichever wood you choose, make sure to select clear stock, since knots will weaken the structure.

Use the leg and rung lengths given for basic reference **(Figure 1)**; their actual measurements should be taken directly off the pattern you make on the work board (see p. 130).

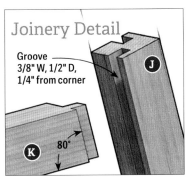

Joinery Detail

Groove
3/8" W, 1/2" D,
1/4" from corner

80°

Order of Work

1. Set up the work board.
2. Groove the post's inside edges.
3. Cut the rungs to length, then cut tongues on the rung ends.
4. Glue up the base and trim the post ends.
5. Make and install the peak assembly.
6. Make and install the trellis assemblies.

Lumber List

- (4) 2" × 6" × 8' cedar
- (2) 1" × 4" × 8' cedar

Figure 1:
Exploded View

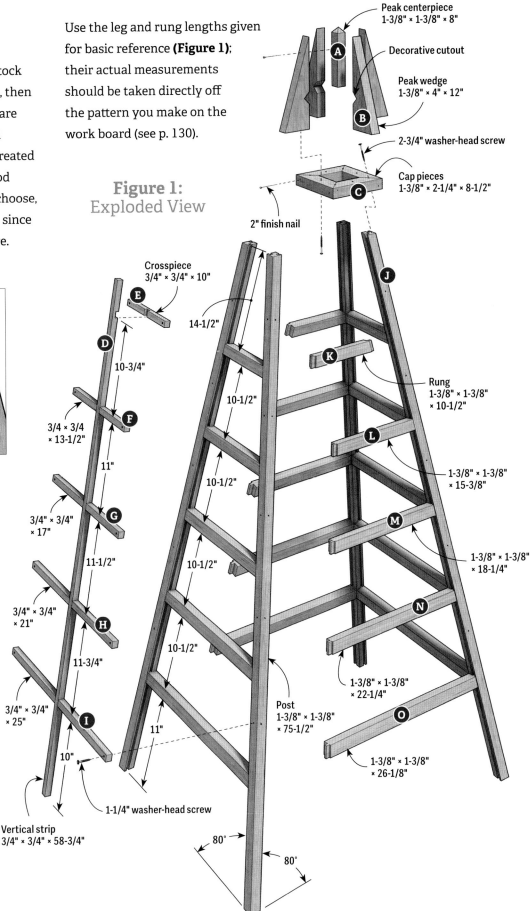

Peak centerpiece
1-3/8" × 1-3/8" × 8"

Decorative cutout

Peak wedge
1-3/8" × 4" × 12"

2-3/4" washer-head screw

Cap pieces
1-3/8" × 2-1/4" × 8-1/2"

2" finish nail

Crosspiece
3/4" × 3/4" × 10"

14-1/2"

10-3/4"

Rung
1-3/8" × 1-3/8"
× 10-1/2"

3/4 × 3/4
× 13-1/2"

10-1/2"

1-3/8" × 1-3/8"
× 15-3/8"

11"

10-1/2"

3/4" × 3/4"
× 17"

1-3/8" × 1-3/8"
× 18-1/4"

11-1/2"

10-1/2"

3/4" × 3/4"
× 21"

11-3/4"

1-3/8" × 1-3/8"
× 22-1/4"

10-1/2"

3/4" × 3/4"
× 25"

Post
1-3/8" × 1-3/8"
× 75-1/2"

1-3/8" × 1-3/8"
× 26-1/8"

10"

1-1/4" washer-head screw

Vertical strip
3/4" × 3/4" × 58-3/4"

11"

80° 80° 80°

Make a work board

With so many angled joints to lay out, cut, and assemble, it helps to have a flat work surface that contains a full-scale pattern of the post (J) and rung (K–O) assemblies you'll be building (Photo A). I made my work board from a piece of inexpensive, 1/2" CDX plywood, coating the work surface with primer so my layout lines were clearly visible. After laying out the posts and rungs, screw cleats down the center of your board at each rung location. You'll use these to clamp rungs in place during assembly. When your work board is complete, record the length of each rung (including tongues), and start cutting your parts to size (Figure 1).

Tongue & groove joints on the router table

To speed and simplify the joinery work, I milled a pair of grooves along the length of each post, then set up a quick way to cut matching tongues in rungs (Photo B). This work gets done on the router table. It's important to offset the grooves in your posts as shown in the sidebar (right) because centered grooves will weaken the post. Make sure to have some scrap rung stock on hand so you can mill some sample tongues and make any adjustments necessary for accurately made joints.

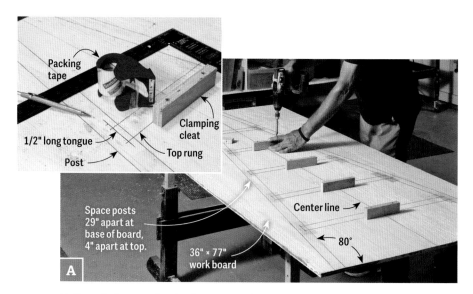

Labels in photo: Packing tape; 1/2" long tongue; Post; Clamping cleat; Top rung; Space posts 29" apart at base of board, 4" apart at top.; Center line; 80°; 36" × 77" work board; A

Full-scale layout. Begin the pattern by marking a centerline down the length of a plywood panel. After laying out the two posts, mark the rung locations, keeping them perpendicular to the centerline. Space the bottom rung 11" from the board's bottom edge. Space the remaining rungs 10-1/2" apart. Lay out 1/2"-long tongues and cover each post/rung joint with packing tape to prevent glue adhesion during assembly (inset photo).

B

Groovy posts. Rout the grooves with a 3/8" straight or spiral flute upcut bit. Adjust the bit height to 1/2", set the fence 1/4" from the cutter, and guide the post against the fence to mill the first groove. Then flip the post end-for-end and rotate it 90° to mill the second groove.

Routing the Tongues

Set up a 3/4" straight bit in the router table, with 1/2" of the cutting width showing outside the fence. Cut an angled backer block that will ride against the fence with a rung clamped in place as shown. Two different bit heights are required to rout offset tongues, with rungs guided at 100° and 80° angles.

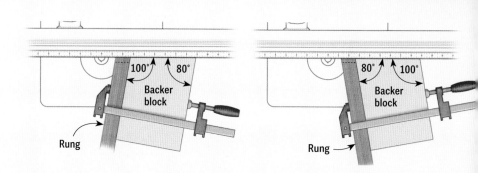

Labels: 100° 80° Backer block Rung; 80° 100° Backer block Rung

4 posts, 20 rungs, 40 joints

Use the work board as an assembly aid to keep parts aligned as you make each tongue-and-groove connection. Titebond III is good to use for this build; it's waterproof and easy to apply, with a longer open time than other outdoor glues. Use a small brush to coat each tongue with glue, and press your post-and-rung **(J, K–O)** joints together to assemble the first ladder frame **(Photo C)**. Then repeat this procedure to complete the opposite frame.

Joining the two ladder frames together demands some nimble maneuvering, because you're installing 10 rungs at once **(Photo D)**. To aid the assembly process, use a chisel or some sandpaper to create a slight chamfer on the end of each rung's tongue. This will avoid snags when getting joints engaged. Trim the post ends **(Photo E, Figure 2)**.

Figure 2:
Compound-Angled
Cutting Guide

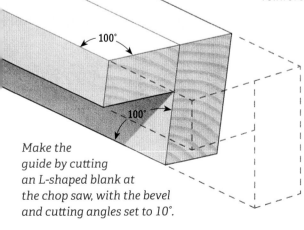

Make the guide by cutting an L-shaped blank at the chop saw, with the bevel and cutting angles set to 10°.

100°

100°

Create a pair of tapered ladders. Start by spreading glue on all the rung tongues and clamping each rung to its clamping cleat. Slide posts into place with open grooves facing up. As you clamp the assembly, make sure that the bottom corner of each post is even with the work board's bottom edge.

Complete the base assembly. Start the glue-up by clamping a set of rungs to their work board cleats, as in the previous step. Then stand both previously assembled frames on edge to engage the tongue-and-groove joints. When the lower set of joints are loosely clamped, you can begin to install the opposite rungs. Tap joints into alignment as necessary, then tighten your clamps. I reinforced each joint with a pair of 1-1/4" stainless steel finish nails.

Use a cutting guide to trim post ends. Make the guide from an L-shaped blank **(Figure 2)**. Clamp it to post tops and bottoms where you want to make your level cuts, and use the angled faces to guide your saw.

Now peak at the top

An obelisk needs a nice crowning touch. The peak detail I came up with is easy to build. It consists of a square cap frame made from four identical mitered pieces **(C)**, and a peak assembly made from four 12"-high wedges **(B)** that surround a pointed centerpiece **(A)** **(Photo F)**. I cut the wedges with my circular saw, then clamped all four together to saw the decorative triangular cutout. Assemble the pieces **(Photo G)**. Attach the peak to the top of the base **(Photo H)**.

F

Use a stop to create a perfect point. Start with a centerpiece 1-3/8" square and at least 10" long. By making four 45° cuts with the butt of the workpiece positioned against a stop block, you can create a perfect point.

G

Screw wedges to the frame. Glue and nail all four wedges to the pointed centerpiece before fastening this assembly to the mitered cap frame.

H

Fasten the cap to the post tops. Position the peak's cap to overlap the posts evenly on all sides, and trace the post ends onto the underside of the cap. This will enable you to drill a pilot hole for a screw that will extend into the "meaty" part of the post, well away from the grooves. Angle your pilot holes slightly to match the 10° post angle. Then fasten the cap to the posts with 2-3/4" washer-head screws.

Trick out your tower with a trellis

Now it's time to put the finishing touches on your obelisk, in the form of four trellis assemblies **(D, E–I)** that overlay the frame. Made from lap-jointed, 3/4"-square stock, these delicate details add visual appeal, while also providing many more anchor points for climbing plants **(Photo I)**. Attach the trellises **(D, E–I)** over each ladder frame face **(Photo J)**.

TIP: If you plan to treat your obelisk to an outdoor finish, apply your finish coats while the base, peak, and trellis assemblies are separate. You'll get more complete coverage, and have a much easier time with finish application.

One pass for four lap joints. I cut the lap joints for the trellis assemblies on the router table, guiding sets of four identical parts (crosspieces and vertical strips) over a 3/4" straight bit with a shop-made miter gauge. To set up for this gang-cut, tape each set of trellis parts together and clamp the assembly to an extended fence on the miter gauge. Bit height should be half the thickness of your parts.

Get your garden ready! I varnished the trellis assemblies and obelisk frame separately before attaching the trellis assemblies with 1-1/4" washer-head screws. To avoid splitting the wood, drill a screw clearance hole 3/4" from the ends of each trellis crosspiece.

Garden Obelisk Supply & Cut List

	Part	Thickness	Width	Length	Qty.
A	Peak centerpiece	1-3/8"	1-3/8"	8"	1
B	Peak wedge	1-3/8"	4"	12"	4
C	Cap pieces	1-3/8"	2-1/4"	8-1/2"	4
D	Vertical lattice strip	3/4"	3/4"	21"	4
E	Lattice crosspiece	3/4"	3/4"	10"	4
F	Lattice crosspiece	3/4"	3/4"	13-1/2"	4
G	Lattice crosspiece	3/4"	3/4"	17"	4
H	Lattice crosspiece	3/4"	3/4"	21"	4
I	Lattice crosspiece	3/4"	3/4"	25"	4
J	Base post	1-3/8"	1-3/8"	75-1/2"	4
K	Base rung	1-3/8"	1-3/8"	10-1/2"	4
L	Base rung	1-3/8"	1-3/8"	15-3/8"	4
M	Base rung	1-3/8"	1-3/8"	18-1/4"	4
N	Base rung	1-3/8"	1-3/8"	22-1/4"	4
O	Base rung	1-3/8"	1-3/8"	26-1/8"	4
	Supplies				
	Washer-head screws			2-3/4"	
	Finish nails			2"	
	Washer-head screws			1-1/4"	
	Finish nails			1-1/4"	

How Good Is Plastic Wood?

Build your next project with lumber that will never decay, crack, warp, or need finishing.

By Asa Christiana

Three years ago I resurfaced my deck with composite boards made from recycled plastic and wood dust. Although I live in the rainy Northwest, a giant Petri dish for moss and mold, the deck still looks as good as the day I installed it. And the only maintenance I've done is a yearly scrub with soap and water.

That got me thinking about using synthetic lumber for other outdoor projects. It took a while, but I tried out the main types of plastic lumber shown here—everything from decking boards skinned with faux wood grain to lightweight PVC trim boards and bright-colored solid plastic stock. All of these varieties offer the advantage of excellent durability under tough outdoor conditions. Plastic lumber will continue to look great while real wood will show signs of damage from moisture, mold, sunlight, and insects. And there's more good news too: You can build almost anything with plastic lumber, using the same power and hand tools you already own. But there are important considerations you'll need to make when switching from real wood to plastic. I'll go over some useful tips about cutting, shaping, and joining the material.

Even though plastic lumber is made almost entirely from bottles, bags, and other products rescued from the waste stream, it's expensive to manufacture. Those costs are passed on to end-users. It's also important to note that plastic boards are typically sold in long lengths. This can be an advantage if you're building a deck, and picking up your material from a local supplier. But if you want small orders or shorter material shipped to you, it can be challenging to find a supplier.

Polyvinyl chloride (PVC)

- Sold in sheets and as 3/4"-thick trim boards. PVC fencing, railing, and decking are also available.
- Trim and sheet stock are available in white only, but these materials can be painted.
- Can be glued using special PVC adhesive.
- More flexible than other types of plastic lumber.

BEST USE: *weatherproof trim and cladding*

Plastic-capped decking boards

- Composite core (recycled plastic and wood dust), with wood-grain cap that protects core from wear, weathering, and mildew.
- Most common dimension is 1" × 5-1/2".
- Many boards come with grooved edges for use with hidden deck fasteners.
- Many wood tones available. Premium decking looks like real wood.

BEST USE: *decking and projects that don't require exposed ends or cut edges*

Uncapped composite decking

- Made from a blend of recycled high-density polyethylene (HDPE) and wood dust/fibers.
- Most boards have a textured surface to simulate wood grain.
- Boards are available in common dimension lumber sizes, and in different wood tones.
- Surface will show slight weathering with age.
- Has the same composition through and through.
- Slightly stiffer than HDPE plastic lumber.

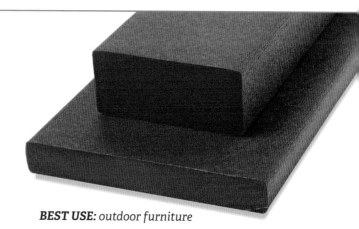

BEST USE: *decking, outdoor railings, and outdoor furniture*

High-density polyethylene (HDPE) lumber

- Sold mostly for commercial use in outdoor furniture, docks, and boardwalks.
- Available in many colors (with UV blockers added to minimize fading).
- Has the same composition and color through and through.
- Lighter than wood-plastic composites.
- More slippery than other plastic lumber.

BEST USE: *outdoor furniture*

Tips for tackling plastic lumber projects

All types of plastic lumber can be worked with most of the same tools you use for woodworking, including (surprisingly) hand and power planes. Sandpaper will clog quickly, so edge-shaping should be done with a mill file, plane, or router.

PVC boards can be joined together with special adhesive, but all other plastic lumber can't be glued. So you'll need to join parts with screws or through-bolted connections.

Plastic lumber expands and contracts in reaction to temperature changes. Movement and strength issues should factor into the design of a plastic wood project. The cutting, shaping, and joinery details shown here will come in handy if you're building with plastic lumber.

Cutting & Routing

Cut smooth and safe. Cut plastic lumber with the same blades you use for wood. It's dense like MDF, but easier on cutting edges.

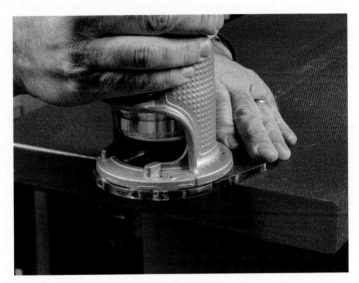

Rout it like real wood. Since plastic lumber lacks grain structure, you can rout without worrying about tear out. To complete more detailed profiles, creep up on the final shape in a series of progressively deeper cuts, as you would with a medium-dense wood like oak.

Design Tips

- Plan to join parts together with bolts or screws.
- Test your design for flex. Plastic decking is designed for joists spaced on 16" or 24" centers. But for furniture like benches and tables, it's smart to mock up supports and make sure your stock won't deflect excessively under anticipated loads.
- Exploit the flexibility of plastic lumber. You can design projects with curved parts. Heating will increase plastic lumber's flexibility.
- For boards with trapped ends, leave a 1/16" gap for every 4' of length.

Joining with Screws & Hardware

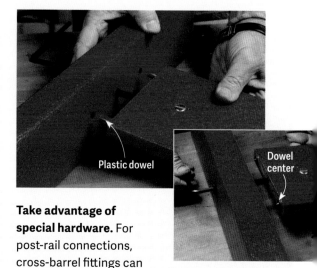

Plastic dowel

Dowel center

Use cabinet screws for solid connections. A low-profile head with an integral washer makes these screws ideal for basic butt joints. To avoid splitting, keep screws at least 3/4" from an edge, and drill clearance holes in the top board. Pilot holes in the base board aren't necessary with these screws, because they have self-drilling tips.

Clamp carefully. Pocket hole joinery works well in plastic lumber, but slick surfaces can easily slip out of alignment. For accurate connections, make sure your parts are secured with clamps before driving screws.

Take advantage of special hardware. For post-rail connections, cross-barrel fittings can be combined with plastic dowels to make strong, attractive joints. Use steel dowel centers to mark plastic dowel locations as you close the joint.

Plugging Holes

Heat gun

Hide holes with a heat gun. Press plugs into place after heating the plug and the hole with a heat gun. No glue is necessary; just make sure both parts have been softened slightly before pressing a plug into place. Once the surface has cooled, trim the plugs slightly proud with a sharp knife, and then plane them flush.

Make plastic plugs. Make short plastic dowels with a plug-cutting bit, then cut them free. Use the dowels in cross-barrel joints, or to hide counterbored or pocket screws.

Wood vs. Wild

Protect your outdoor projects with this handy survival guide.

By Robert J. Settich

N one of us would ever dream of sending our children out into the snow without a proper coat, boots, and mittens. Yet some people callously shove their woodworking creations out the door to face Arctic blasts, blistering heat, and torrential rain. And while cruelty to wood won't land you in prison, it will definitely peel years away from your project's life expectancy and serve a death sentence to its good looks.

To help save your outdoor projects from abuse, we developed a condensed survival guide covering wood and manufactured panels, fasteners, adhesives, and finishes.

Domestic softwoods

Domestic softwoods with natural decay resistance include western red cedar, cypress, and redwood. Shipping costs usually dictate which species is available in your area. All are lightweight and easy to work. However, realize that these species are particularly soft softwoods and therefore are susceptible to surface damage by a stray hammer blow or collision with brick, concrete, and other unforgiving surfaces.

Western red cedar

Redwood

Cypress

Mahogany

Teak

Ipe

Tropical hardwoods

Tropical hardwoods such as teak and ipe have high density and natural decay resistance, two factors that recommend them for outdoor furniture. But these woods can be hard to find and usually have eye-popping price tags. Genuine mahogany (not lauan) is another decay-resistant wood that is lower in both density and price.

White oak

White oak is an excellent domestic hardwood for exterior projects because its closed cell structure inhibits moisture absorption. That's why it works for everything from whiskey barrels to porch swings.

White oak

Choices for Outdoor Wood

	Weight (lb/ft³)	Hardness	Workability
Mahogany*	33	Medium	Easy to work. Moderate blunting effect on cutting edges.
Teak*	40	Hard	Silica content dulls cutting edges. Glue fresh-cut edges or clean with naphtha to eliminate oil contamination.
Ipe*	67	Very hard	Moderate dulling effect. Glue fresh-cut edges or clean with naphtha to eliminate oil contamination.
Western Red Cedar*	20	Soft	Minimal dulling effect. Iron contact will create black stains.
Redwood*	26	Soft	Minimal dulling effect. Use sharp cutters to reduce splintering. Iron contact will create black staining. Predrill holes to avoid splitting.
Cypress*	29	Moderate	Minimal dulling effect. Works well with hand and power tools. Accepts finishes readily.
White Oak*	47	Hard	Moderate dulling effect. Iron will create black stains.

Exposure to dust can cause an allergic reaction, such as nose and eye irritation, asthma, and dermatitis. Repeated exposure to dust can cause sensitivity. Future exposure can cause immediate allergic reaction.

Pressure-treated lumber

Pressure-treated lumber involves injection of a chemical. Chromated copper arsenate (CCA), a previous choice, has been replaced by alkaline copper quaternary (ACQ), with slightly different formulations tailored to various wood species, the most common being pines. The end of each board should have a stapled tag that identifies the treating company, chemical, year, and whether the amount of chemical retained in the wood makes it suitable for ground contact or only above-ground use. Be sure to select fasteners that can stand up to ACQ's corrosive properties.

Exterior-grade plywood

Exterior-grade plywood is excellent for many outdoor projects. If plywood qualifies for exterior use, it will have the word "exterior" as part of the stamp that also identifies the face veneer grades. This indicates that exterior-rated adhesive bonds the plies. Pressure-treated plywood is another great choice for outside projects.

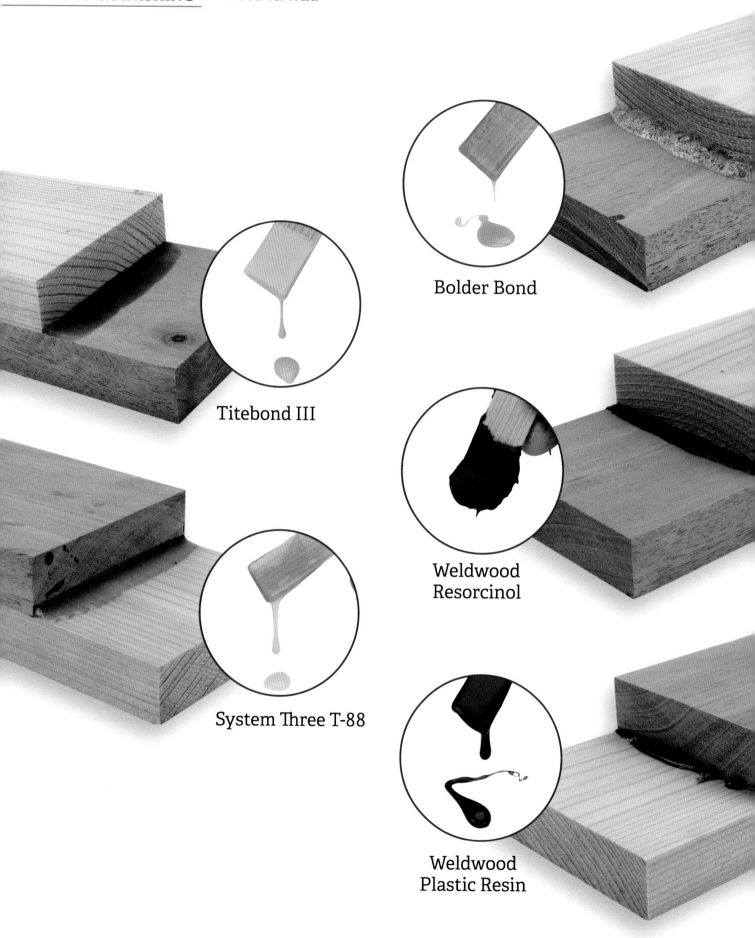

Titebond III

System Three T-88

Bolder Bond

Weldwood
Resorcinol

Weldwood
Plastic Resin

Long-lasting exterior adhesives

Modern adhesives routinely perform chores that would have been considered nearly miraculous a generation ago. In fact, Titebond III is the first one-part waterproof glue that offers water cleanup. It's suitable for many outdoor projects but inexpensive enough that many woodworkers also use it for their indoor projects.

TIP: Polyurethane glue fills gaps, but don't consider that an invitation to produce sloppy joinery. Work joints to the same tolerances as for your indoor work, aiming for surfaces that slide together with minimal pressure.

The chart below gives you fast facts on the key types of adhesives suitable for outdoor projects ranging from birdhouses to boats. In addition, you'll find a wide range of products within the epoxy family to suit specialized applications. Epoxy putty, for example, is both an adhesive as well as a gap filler that can plug a knothole.

Some other useful outdoor bonding products include construction adhesives: Loctite PL and Liquid Nails are two well-known and widely available brands.

TIP: Quick-set epoxy allows you to unclamp your project sooner, but it has only about half the ultimate strength of the slower-setting formula. If you have a little patience up front, your project will be stronger in the long run.

Get furniture out of puddles. Hard-wearing plastic glides elevate outdoor furniture legs above water so it can't wick into the end grain.

Choices for Outdoor Glue

Brand/Generic	Open Time*	Set Time**	Solvent	Notes
Titebond III / waterproof yellow	10 min.	1 hour	Water	Not for continuous submersion or structural applications.
System Three T-88 Epoxy / two-part epoxy	10 min. Varies w/hardener	6 hours	Lacquer thinner	Gap filler. You can add fillers such as sawdust.
Bolder Bond / polyurethane	20 min.	1–4 hours	Denatured alcohol	Wear gloves to protect your hands. Easy to sand or scrape when dry.
Weldwood Resorcinol / resorcinol formaldehyde	30 minutes	10 hours	Water	Suitable for even marine applications. Observe ventilation and safety warnings.
Weldwood Plastic Resin / powdered plastic resin	20–30 min.	12 hours	Water	Long open time is useful for complex assemblies. Bond has very good structural strength.

Open time = maximum duration from initial mixing or spreading until project is clamped.

**Set time = minimum time that project is in clamps before gentle handling.*

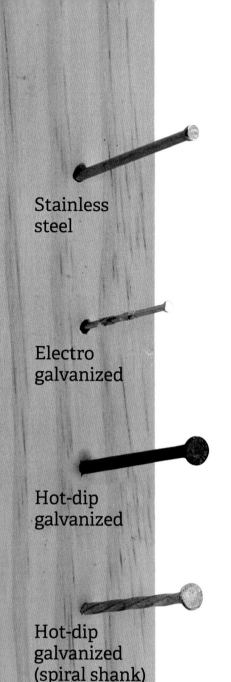

Stainless
steel

Electro
galvanized

Hot-dip
galvanized

Hot-dip
galvanized
(spiral shank)

Outdoor-rated fasteners

The chemical properties that make
certain woods naturally rot-resistant
can also attack fasteners, causing
corrosion that can weaken joints
and cause unsightly staining. The
powerful chemicals employed for
pressure-treating lumber can be even
more reactive with fasteners, making
your choices even more critical.

*TIP: Stainless steel is softer than
ordinary steel, so maintaining identical
strength in shear means that you
need to buy screws with a larger
diameter. As a rule of thumb, go up
one or two gauges. For example, if
you would ordinarily use a #6 steel
screw, upsize it to #8 in stainless. The
same upscale thinking applies to
stainless steel bolts and lag screws.*

There are two broad categories of
outdoor-rated fasteners. One type
uses a corrosion-resistant material
for the fastener itself, and the
other relies on a protective plating
or coating to shield a steel body.

Using a metal that resists
corrosion, such as stainless steel
or brass, offers more dependable
performance than galvanizing and
other surface treatments that can be
easily damaged by abrasion or impact.

*TIP: Drilling pilot and shank-
clearance holes helps prevent screws
from splitting your lumber. Splits
aren't just unsightly; they also open
the wood to water penetration.*

Stainless steel screws are
generally suitable for outdoor
projects, but not all alloys are truly
stainless in every application. As a
general guide, select the 316 stainless
alloy for marine applications, but
choose among the less-expensive
302, 304, or 305 screws for general
exterior projects. Screws in the 200

Weather-Resistant Coatings

Ceramic   Epoxy   Kreg Blue-Kote   Zinc plated

series use alloys that cut back on the expensive metals, saving money but compromising corrosion resistance. To be on the safe side, choose screws that are clearly identified as compatible with your project's building material. **Stainless steel nails** are available but can be tough to find.

Silicon bronze screws have corrosion resistance that is tough enough for boat-building chores: the 651 alloy, for example. As with stainless steel, there are various alloys, so it pays to read carefully and ask questions before you buy.

Aluminum screws as well as those made from **solid brass** have excellent corrosion resistance but both of these materials are quite soft, so drilling pilot holes is an absolute necessity. You'll also need to carefully monitor your torque when driving to avoid snapping the screw in two.

Zinc-plated screws as well as **coated screws** offer good exterior performance at a budget-conscious price. Kreg Blue-Kote screws claim a rust-resistant performance that's 400% better than their former zinc-coated screws. However, these screws are not recommended for use with ACQ-treated lumber.

Epoxy and ceramic coatings that resist corrosion are typically used for **deck screws**, and you'll often find a range of colors to help them blend into their surroundings. Read the box before you buy, especially if you're working with ACQ lumber.

TIP: *When you use fasteners that touch each other, such as bolts, washers, and nuts, make sure that all of the components are the same material. Mixing materials in the presence of moisture creates a tiny electrical current (galvanic reaction) that hastens corrosion.*

Galvanized nails, bolts, and lag screws utilize a zinc coating to resist corrosion. Electro-galvanizing produces a smooth plated surface for air-driven nails as well as the manually driven version. Hot-dip galvanizing produces a thicker but rougher surface coating on hand-driven nails. Deck and siding nails with a twisted or ringed shank offer excellent pull-out resistance.

Corrosion-Resistant Metals

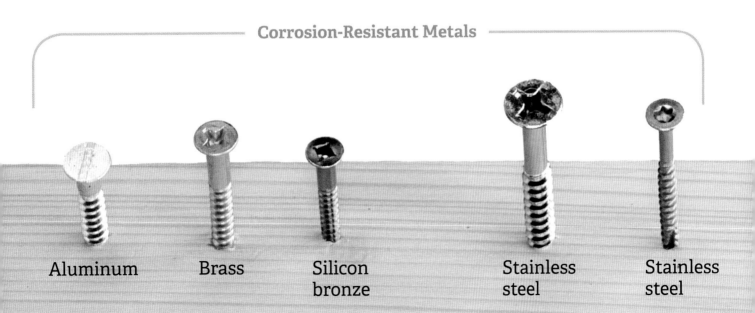

Aluminum   Brass   Silicon bronze   Stainless steel   Stainless steel

Choosing Wood for Outdoor Projects

When it comes to the great outdoors, not all woods are created equal.

By Udo Schmidt

The choice of wood you make for outdoor projects can mean years of enjoyment or potential disappointment. Fortunately, there are several species in North America very suitable for outdoor projects. Finding the right wood depends on the woodworker's location and pocketbook. Some species are readily available in lumberyards—even in home improvement warehouses—while others are not available in commercial trade, but can be obtained from local sawmills.

Choose a resilient wood for outdoor projects. With proper care and the right choices of wood and finish, outdoor furniture can withstand conditions such as moisture and bugs.

Heartwood & Sapwood: The Difference

In a living tree, the heartwood is for support and doesn't conduct water or store food. In contrast, sapwood contains both living and dead cells and transports water and nutrients from the roots to the leaves. The thickness of the sapwood varies greatly among species, from only 1/2" in black locust to up to 6" in hickories and maples. After several years of growth, the cells become inactive and increase in extractive content like resins, gums, waxes, oils, polyphenols, and tannins and become heartwood. Heartwood is usually darker in color than sapwood because of its higher level of extractives, which also makes wood from the heartwood of some species highly resistant to decay.

Heartwood can be even tougher. The reddish heartwood of eastern red cedar is very decay-resistant.

When buying wood that will be exposed to the elements, look for wood that is decay resistant, insect resistant, and weather resistant. Approximately 10% of North American lumber production is used to replace damaged wood on structures or other element-exposed wooden objects. Regardless of the species, the sapwood part of any wood has no natural resistance to decay. The first thing to do is to understand the difference between heartwood and sapwood (see sidebar above).

Another important aspect to consider is the growth ring arrangement. A good example is western red cedar. If the growth rings are more than 1/8" apart, this wood is considered only moderately resistant to decay. With decay-resistant species, the closer the growth rings, the more decay-resistant the wood.

The main difference in wooden indoor or outdoor projects is the moisture content to which the wood will equalize. Indoors, wood's moisture content fluctuates between 6% in winter and 12% in summer. However, outdoors wood seldom goes below a moisture content of 12%, except in dry desert conditions. It can also absorb moisture to over 20% (up to the species' fiber saturation point) during a period of humid or wet conditions. In other words, moisture content usually fluctuates more in outdoor wood than indoor wood. This means that outdoor wood swells and shrinks in greater dimensions than wood used indoors. Using kiln-dried wood for outdoor projects is not necessary; however, lumber in home improvement stores is sometimes sold as kiln-dried. Most likely this wood is still well above its fiber saturation point and should be air-dried before using.

Regardless of the wood you choose, there are a few points to consider if you want to eliminate or retard decay.

Apply several coats of finish to the end grain of the wood before assembling the project. The end grain is more susceptible to moisture absorption and will check and split long before the other parts of the wood. If this is not possible, apply several extra coats of finish on all exposed end grain after assembly.

Keep your project out of direct sunlight and weather. This dramatically reduces maintenance. For instance, an Adirondack chair located under a covered porch might need only a coat of finish every two years. But if the chair is exposed to the elements, it needs two coats a year to keep it looking new.

Don't bury bare wood in the ground (e.g., fence posts). Instead, build a concrete foundation and paint the buried part in heavy roof tar or creosote. Concrete traps moisture around wood much longer because it cannot drain naturally.

Keep water and snow away from your project. Don't let a chair sit in a puddle of water or let snow lay on play equipment.

Even though most of the species mentioned here are highly resistant to decay, that doesn't mean that they are also resistant to insects. For instance, teak is resistant to termites, but not to the marine borer. If you anticipate insect damage to your project, a product called Bug

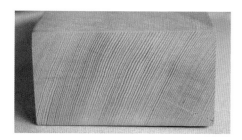

Growth rings indicate resistance. Tight growth rings show decay resistance in this old-growth cedar.

Juice can be added to the last coat of finish. A 1.66 oz. bottle is mixed to one gallon of paint, stain, or oil.

Highly decay-resistant hardwoods are not just scientifically classified as hardwoods, they are hard woods. These species include black locust, osage orange, and red mulberry. They are very hard to work with, but are a good choice for projects that have ground contact. Osage orange is one of the densest of the native species. With a specific gravity of .85 at 12% moisture content, it weighs over 4-1/2 lb per board foot.

Native softwoods most often used for outdoor projects include cedar, redwood, and cypress. They are all easy to work with and have low shrinkage properties. Western red cedar is the wood most frequently used for outside applications like house siding and decking. Of the exotics, teak is the typical choice for outdoor furniture and marine products. Among the highly decay-resistant species, it is also the most expensive.

Teak has many unique characteristics which make it the preferred choice for projects exposed

Staining

Stains in wood are caused by minute parasitic organisms that need water, warm temperatures, and oxygen to grow. Fungi feed on sugar in the sapwood of logs and lumber with a moisture content of more than 22% or when the relative humidity is more than 92%. The affected wood is then sap stained.

Blue stain is the most common. The discoloration varies in color depending on the infecting organism, wood species, and moisture situation. Blue stain shows as bluish to bluish-black or gray to brown. The affected areas can be spotty or streaky. In severe cases, the entire sapwood is discolored.

Although sap stains seldom change the strength properties of wood, heavy sap stains reduce the toughness of the wood and its ability to withstand shock. Stained areas also have a higher water absorption capacity and therefore are more susceptible to other organisms such as decay fungi. Even though decay fungi are not a stain, they live and thrive under the same conditions as mold and sap stain.

Temperatures of 75° to 85° are optimal. However, fungal growth slows to half the optimal rate at temperatures of 32° to 50° and the organisms die at temperatures over 130°.

Another characteristic of fungi is that they can go dormant for long periods of time. Only high temperatures and chemical treatments kill them. Any fungal stain is permanent and cannot be removed or lightened by chemicals like bleach or oxalic acid.

Watch out. Even though stains and mildew are not the same fungi as decay organisms, they indicate that conditions are right for decay to begin.

to the elements. With a specific gravity of about .5 to .6, it is as dense as native oak and has similar workability. Teak has one of the lowest shrinkage properties of all wood species, which makes it extremely stable. Its natural oil also makes it a preferred choice for an unfinished, weathered-look project. Unfortunately, depending on its growth location,

teak can have a very high silica content. Silica has a dulling effect on all cutting and machining tools.

By choosing the right wood, and with the proper finish and occasional care, your outdoor project should bring you years of enjoyment.

Outdoor Finishes

Choose the right finish to dress your outdoor woodwork for success.

By Derek Richmond

When it rains, it pours. So you put on a raincoat—or go inside. And when the snows come, you bundle up. Sunny? A pair of sunglasses and maybe some SPF lotion. But your outdoor furniture and other woodwork don't have such luxuries. Those pieces rely on you to store them inside or undercover, and when that's not practical, to apply and maintain a protective finish.

While no product will completely protect your projects from the rain, snow, and sun, choosing the right finish and applying it the right way is a critical opening gambit in the uphill battle of keeping your woodwork lasting long and looking beautiful. After all, the finish has to balance protection from the elements with an element of simplicity in both application and renewal. As you'll see in the following pages, those

finishes that offer better protection at the beginning can also be more difficult to maintain and refinish.

And maintaining an outdoor finish may be necessary, but it doesn't have to be evil. The trick is picking the right finish, then knowing how and—just as importantly—how often to maintain that finish to protect your projects and keep your wood looking good season after season.

Oil-based varnishes

Varnish has come to be a catch-all term for any number of film-forming finishes. Most oil-based "varnishes" consist of a drying oil (usually tung or linseed), a resin (typically alkyd or polyurethane) and a solvent (mineral spirits). Varying the type and ratio of those components affects characteristics of the protective layer formed by the film. Exterior oil-based varnishes—some manufacturers dub them "spar" from the days of tall-masted ships—contain a greater percentage of oils than their interior counterparts. This formulation means exterior varnish remains more flexible when cured, lessening the likelihood of it cracking or peeling from seasonal wood movement. Frequently, these finishes also contain UV blockers that inhibit the sun's ultraviolet rays from degrading the wood beneath. The trade-off is that exterior varnishes aren't as hard or durable as interior formulations. Depending on the weather, a well-applied exterior varnish will last 2–3 years before it begins to look chalky. When it does, sand the surface and apply a fresh coat. Do this before the finish develops cracks; otherwise you may have to sand down to bare wood. Oil-based varnishes, which impart an amber hue to the wood, can be applied by brush or spray. When applying to bare wood, it's often wise to thin the initial coat with mineral spirits (up to 50% with some products) to promote good adhesion.

Exterior varnish for multi-layered protection. For maximum protection, some manufacturers recommend applying 7–8 coats of their exterior varnishes. Thin as directed and allow to dry before scuff-sanding between coats. Clean up with mineral spirits.

Water-based varnishes

These film-forming finishes are also resin-based (alkyd, urethane, and/or acrylic) but use water as their solvent, making them environmentally friendlier and easier to clean up. Like their oil-based cousins, the outdoor formulations form a weather- and UV-resistant film that remains flexible. Although milky-white as a liquid, they dry clear with no amber cast. This tends to flatten the color and grain rather than enhance it the way an oil-based varnish does. Staining first can help, as can using amber-colored additives made for the purpose. Water-based varnishes can be applied over other non-oil-based finishes such as milk paint to add gloss and durability, but be sure to check for compatibility first. To apply a water-based finish, first raise the wood grain with distilled water and then lightly sand away the raised fibers before brushing or spraying on 3–4 thin coats. Allow each coat to dry thoroughly, then sand and recoat. Clean up with water.

Water-based varnish gives toughness on top. A water-based varnish adds protection and gloss to bare wood and painted surfaces. Here it's being sprayed on a white oak ladder-ball game.

Sealers: Keeping water out

While they are not a complete finish, sealers enjoy a symbiotic relationship with film-forming finishes such as varnish, enhancing their protection. Some sealers consist of two parts—a resin and a hardener. Mixing them creates a thin epoxy with an open time sufficient to allow brushing or spraying. Other brands are single-part liquids. Both soak deeply into the wood with the same goal: preventing water penetration and therefore rot. Sealers don't provide UV protection, and need a topcoat to prevent sun damage and weathering. For optimum protection, seal all project parts (except glue-joint surfaces) with 2–3 coats after cutting the parts to size, but before assembling them. Once your piece is together, topcoat as normal. This added step may well be worth it for significant projects that will be left out in all conditions. Or consider using sealers locally, where they provide the most benefit, such as on the end-grain feet of outdoor furniture.

Keep your feet dry. Sealers penetrate wood and fill pores to keep water out, making them particularly useful on the feet of outdoor furniture.

Milk paint: Color & protection

Traditional milk paint is a combination of lime (or borax), a pigment, and casein, a protein found in milk. These ingredients make it non-toxic, biodegradable, and fume-free. Milk paint also holds up well outside, and is nearly impossible to remove. Available in powdered form, you mix it with warm water to the consistency of a melted milkshake, then brush or wipe it onto sanded wood surfaces. Thinning it with extra water creates a more rustic "washed" look. The available colors tend toward barn reds, colonial blues, and linen whites. Mix it in small batches, as it doesn't keep more than a day.

One manufacturer offers premixed "milk" paints in similar, muted colors fortified with added acrylic resins. These water-based paints come in cans and share many of the non-toxic qualities of the traditional powders.

Whether powdered or pre-mixed, milk paint provides a smooth, velvety finish without a sheen. Several coats may be required for complete coverage, which also provides UV protection. Adding a water-based varnish over milk paint will help maintain its color, enhance UV protection, and add some gloss.

Brighten up. Add a splash of color to your outdoor projects with milk paint. Whether powdered or premixed, these coatings offer protection from both sun and weather.

Stains: Perfect for structures

Stains represent some of the most effective and easily applied outdoor finishes around. While generally intended for decking and siding, they are also appropriate for most outdoor projects. Available as water-based, oil-based, or as a hybrid of both, stains come in variety of colors and in three types: transparent, semitransparent, and solid. Transparent stains contain the least amount of pigment, which allows the grain of the wood to show through, but which offers less UV protection. Transparent stains won't peel, but typically need to be recoated yearly. Semi-transparent stains offer a little more protection and longevity (typically 2–3 years, with no peeling) while still allowing the wood's grain to show. Solid (or opaque) stains very closely mimic paint, although they do tend to show the grain's texture. They offer the most protection and longest lifespan (5–7 years) but can peel if the surfaces aren't properly prepared. Oil-based stains tend to give the wood a more natural look. Water-based stains, with their acrylic resins, are better at resisting UV damage, but can raise the grain. The new hybrid stains combine the characteristics of oil- and water-based products. All of the choices can be applied by brushing, rolling, or spraying. Clean up according to the base solvent.

Stains give enhanced protection and color. These sample cedar boards show the spectrum from transparent to solid stain in the same color. Stains are a balancing act, with more opaque stains offering better protection, and more transparent stains showing the wood's inherent beauty.

Penetrating oils: Working from within

Unlike film finishes, such as varnishes and paints, which form a barrier on the wood's surface, penetrating oils soak into the wood and do their work from within. While there are myriad formulations with names such as "timber," "teak," and "outdoor" oil, they all have some similar characteristics. Oils maintain a natural (though darkened) look without adding a glossy coating, so there's nothing to peel or flake. The flip side is that oils offer less protection than film-forming finishes, and eventually the wood will gray from exposure. Outdoor oils usually incorporate UV-blockers and some contain heat stabilizers and mildew inhibitors. Of all the available outdoor finishes, oil is undoubtedly the easiest to apply: wipe or brush on liberally, recoating every 6–12 months to maintain the protective barrier. Fortunately there's usually no need to sand before reapplying additional coats.

Wipe on, soak, wipe off. Thoroughly stir the finish, then wipe it on with a rag, let it soak in per the manufacturer's direction, and wipe off. A coat or two will do, since penetrating oil does not build a film.

Restoring Outdoor Projects

Add years to the life of your lawn and patio furniture.

By Marlen Kemmet

Year after year, outdoor furniture pieces take a brutal beating from Mother Nature in the form of intense sunlight, temperature extremes, moisture, windblown dirt and pollen, and insects. To wage the good fight and extend the life of these cherished pieces, follow along as I take you step by step through the rehab of an Adirondack chair, solving common problems that afflict most outdoor projects, and extending its useful life.

Can this project be saved?

Over time, all wood projects reach the point of no return. But, in the case of this Adirondack chair, it was worth the time and effort for me to restore this weathered old friend. How can you tell if an outdoor project has passed its prime?

For starters, check for severe wood rot, warping, or large checks or cracks in individual parts. Looks can be deceiving. At first blush, the Adirondack chair looked destined for the landfill. But underneath the grit, lichen, and grime was a perfectly functional piece in need of a little TLC. Although the wood appeared badly weathered, a little sanding and scraping on the bottom side of a seat slat revealed sound lumber.

Next, check the joints for further rot, looseness, and hardware issues that undermine the project's structural integrity. Are replacement parts or new hardware in order? With seating of any kind, these are critical for safety. Is the finish flaking or otherwise compromised? If what you are facing is a lost cause, you may find it cheaper and far more time-saving to simply build a sturdier replacement.

Common fixes for failing furniture

After assessing your furniture piece and deciding that it's worth saving, develop an action plan. Use these strategies to remedy a variety of problems.

Before

Clean the piece

Problem

Lichen, mold, weathering, and encrusted dirt have attacked the project, detracting from its appearance and leading to decay.

Solution

Depending upon the severity of the degradation you have two choices. For projects like the chair, I recommend pressure-washing the entire piece at a low setting using a wide-nozzle tip on the wand **(Photo A)**. Rinse the entire piece first. Then, power-wash it with a commercial solution to clean and brighten the wood. Or, save a few bucks by mixing your own solution. I used one quart of household bleach, one-third cup of powdered laundry soap, and three quarts of water. A raincoat, safety glasses, and gloves come in handy for protection against splatter.

   If you don't have access to a power washer, spray the piece down with a garden hose and scrub the grime off **(Photo B)**. Avoid a wire brush, as the hard, stiff bristles may cause deep scratches in the wood, which will have to be sanded.

Power wash. For badly damaged pieces, a power-washer and a cleaning solution provide the first step.

Scrub. A stiff-bristled brush and lots of elbow grease clean entrenched grime at little cost.

Power-Washing Pointers

When power-washing outdoor furniture, start with the lowest setting, hold the nozzle end of the wand about 18" away to start, and move closer if necessary. Too high of a pressure setting or a tip held too close can damage the wood, much like sandblasting. Power-washer spray tips come in different spray patterns, with the range spanning from 0° to 40°. The wider the angle, the more surface area covered, but with less impact.

Disassemble for a complete restoration

Problem

Grit and grime have infiltrated joints and other hard-to-get-at nooks and crannies. In some cases, a part or two may need to be replaced. Disassembly may be your best course of action, but getting all of the parts back in their proper location may be an issue.

Solution

Many outdoor projects, such as the Adirondack chair, are simply screwed together, making disassembly easy. But this could result in a jumble of similar pieces. To reattach the parts later without puzzling over where they go and for proper screw hole alignments, grab a camera and take numerous reference photos before you take the project apart. Label the parts, and transfer the labels onto printed copies of the photos. Also, keep a tape measure handy to record key part locations on the photos **(Photo C)**. Re-mark any sanded parts.

TIP: Print a digital image of the furniture piece and label important measurements for later reassembly. You can also use pieces of blue painter's tape affixed to chair parts for quick reference later.

Take notes. Measure and record important spacing dimensions for ease in reassembling the chair later.

Level rough wood surfaces

Problem

Raised grain surfaces are rough and full of ridges due, in part, to the different wear rates of earlywood and latewood softwoods.

Solution

After the furniture piece has thoroughly dried (I left the chair in direct sunlight for two days), it's time to smooth rough surfaces. Since the chair disassembled easily, sanding the individual parts proved much easier than trying to sand the assembled chair. It also allowed me to sand mating areas and edges.

To minimize sanding time, you can use a variety of portable sanders to tackle different tasks. For larger flat surfaces, use an orbital sander to cover a lot of ground fast. For curved edges, a palm sander is my tool of choice **(Photo D)**. For tight areas on an assembled project, hand-sanding may be your only choice.

TIP: Use a moisture meter for an accurate reading of an outdoor project's dampness level before attempting to sand or apply finish. Woods, such as cedar and redwood, should be 12% (or less) moisture content.

Smooth the surfaces. Rely on a palm sander to smoothly sand curved edges, such as this leg part.

Fill cracks & gaps

Problem

Moisture in the wood of an outdoor piece causes the fibers to swell and then contract as they dry out, resulting in cracks and checks along the grain and at the ends of parts.

Solution

The best way to avoid cracking and checking is to seal the wood project properly during construction to keep moisture out, and then reseal it regularly. When cracks occur on weathered pieces, fill them **(Photo E)**, and then sand the pieces smooth once the filler dries. For minute cracks, filler will do, but for damaged areas requiring repair or buildup, use a two-part epoxy-based putty. The closer you can shape the putty to the original surface, the less sanding you'll have to do after the putty hardens.

TIP: For optimal results, choose putty that dries hard with minimal shrinkage, such as a two-part epoxy-based putty developed for exterior use.

E

Fill the cracks. A putty knife helps you push and smooth the filler into minor splits and checks. Sand the area smooth.

Replace suspect hardware

Problem

Rusty or broken screws, as well as stripped screw holes, cause joints to fail; hinges can wear out, requiring full hardware replacement.

Solution

Extract broken or rusty screws using a screw extractor **(Photo F)**. When replacing old hardware, don't skimp on the quality of screws, hinges, and other metal fasteners.

To eliminate exposed screw heads that are both unsightly and serve to collect water, counterbore the holes and plug the screws **(Photo G)**.

For more information on hardware for outdoor use, see p. 144–145.

TIP: If replacing old screws and stripped holes, go up a gauge when returning to the holes. Go with a #10 gauge instead of #8 for a tighter fit.

F

Remove a broken screw. Use a screw extractor to minimize damage to the surrounding wood.

G

Trim plugs. A flush-trim saw works best for trimming plugs even with the surrounding surface.

Replace damaged parts

Problem

While salvaging your outdoor project, you encountered parts that proved beyond repair.

Don't let a few badly damaged pieces prevent you from salvaging the project.

Solution

For the chair, the horizontal armrests took the brunt of weathering. I could have spent a fair amount of effort and materials filling and sanding the badly damaged pieces, but it proved more economical to simply create new armrests.

To make identical part replacements, I removed the old armrests and used one (they're mirror images of each other) as a template to trace its shape onto 1/2" plywood. I bandsawed the plywood to shape and

sanded the edges smooth to create a routing template. I then traced the armrest's outline onto two 3/4"-thick pieces of cedar and bandsawed the armrest blanks to shape **(Photo H)**. I adhered the template to a rough-cut armrest with double-faced tape. Using a flush-trim pattern cutting bit at my table-mounted router and guiding off the template, I cleaned up the edges **(Photo I)**.

H

Trace the part. Mark the blank slightly larger by holding the pencil upright when running it along the original part.

TIP: To mark a blank slightly larger than the needed finished shape of the replacement piece, hold the pencil perfectly upright, riding the shank of the pencil against the original furniture piece. This will mark the blank 1/8" larger than the original and provide just enough extra edge stock to be routed when using the template to rout the armrest to final shape.

I

Shape the piece. Rout the replacement part to final shape with a pattern-cutting bit and plywood template.

Seal & finish for long life

Problem

Unsealed wood absorbs moisture, resulting in a many deterioration issues, from rapid graying due to intense sunlight to moisture penetration and accelerated rot and decay.

Solution

Now that you've replaced parts, filled cracks, and sanded the project smooth, finish the project to protect it from the elements and to keep it looking good. Soak the ends of

parts that are in direct ground contact with a preservative such as penetrating oil finish **(Photo J)**.

Now, finish your piece. I applied two coats of General Finishes Sage Green Milk Paint **(Photo K)**. For more information, see p. 151.

see p. 151.

TIP: With a disassembled outdoor project, seal and finish the parts before reassembling them. If the parts of a project are glued together and cannot be removed, do the needed prep work and apply the finish to the assembled piece.

J

Seal the feet. To protect feet bottoms from future rot, soak them in a container of preservative prior to finishing.

K

Apply finish. Milk paint (here, acrylic latex) is self-sealing and does not require a primer. If your project allows it, painting individual parts yields the best results.

Contributors

A-Frame Planter

Author: Tim Snyder

Lead photographer: Paul Anthony

Step photographer: Randy O'Rourke

Illustrator: Christopher Mills

Adirondack Glider

Author: Robert J. Settich

Builder: Bill Sands

Adirondack Table & Footstool

Author: Bill Sands

Photographer: Morehead Photography

Illustrator: Christopher Mills

Arbor Gate

Author/Designer: Alan Turner

Designer/Photographer: Mario Rodriguez

Illustrator: Chuck Lockhart

Build a Bench

Author: Joe Hurst-Wajszczuk

Designer: Andy Rae

Photographer: Ralph Lee Anderson

Illustrator: Frank Rohrbach III

Choosing Woods for Outdoor Projects

Author/Photographer: Udo Schmidt

Lead photographer: Elenathewise, istockphoto.com

Classic Adirondack Chair

Author: Lori Mossor

Illustrator: Shane Wiersma

Easy-Breezy Porch Swing

Author: Jim Harrold

Designer/Builder: Gary Carter

Photographer: Jim Osborn

Origins of the Adirondack Chair

Author: Tim Snyder

Photographer, top image: Spruce Bay Inn

Photographer, bottom images:
The Best Adirondack Chair Co.

Garden Arbor

Author/Designer: Alan Turner

Designer/Photographer: Mario Rodriguez

Illustrator: Chuck Lockhart

Garden Bench

Author/Step photographer: Andy Rae

Lead photographer: Ken Brady

Garden Obelisk

Author: Tim Snyder

Photographer: Randy O'Rourke

Illustrator: John Hartman

High-Top Patio Chair

Author: Chris Spoerer

Lead photographer: Larry Hamel-Lambert

Step photographer: Ben Blackmar

Illustrator: Christopher Mills

High-Top Patio Table

Author: Chris Spoerer

Lead photographer: Larry Hamel-Lambert

Step photographer: Ben Blackmar

Illustrator: Christopher Mills

How Good is Plastic Wood?

Author/Photographer: Asa Christiana

Octagonal Picnic Table

Author: Bill Sands

Photographer: Jim Osborn

Illustrator: Christopher Mills

Outdoor Finishes

Author: Derek Richmond

Photographer: John Hamel

Outdoor Table & Benches

Author/Step photographer: Ken Burton

Lead photographer: Paul Anthony

Illustrator: John Hartman

Potting Bench

Author/Photographer: Ken Burton

Illustrator: Christopher Mills

Restoring Outdoor Projects

Author: Marlen Kemmet

Photographer: Doug Hetherington

The Haycock Adirondack

Author/Photographer: Paul Anthony

Author: Ken Burton

Designer: Ric Hanisch

Illustrator: Christopher Mills

Wood vs. Wild

Author: Robert J. Settich

Lead photographer: Doug Hetherington

Publisher: Paul McGahren
Editorial Director: Kerri Grzybicki
Design & Layout: Bobby Schehl

Cedar Lane Press
PO Box 5424
Lancaster, PA 17606-5424

Paperback ISBN: 978-1-950934-82-9
ePub ISBN: 978-1-950934-83-6

Library of Congress Control Number: 2021948469

Printed in the United States of America
10   9   8   7   6   5   4   3   2   1

Note: The following list contains names used in *Building Outdoor Furniture* that may be registered with the United States Copyright Office: Bolder Bond; Cabot (Australian Timber Oil); Epifanes; Festool (Domino); General Finishes; HeadLOK; Kreg (Blue-Kote); Levi Innovations (Swing-Mate); Liquid Nails; Loctite (PL); Osmo; Sikkens (Cetol SRD); System Three; Titebond; UC Coatings (Seal Once Nano); Valspar; Walla Walla Environmental (Bug Juice); Watco; Weldwood.

To learn more about Cedar Lane Press books, or to find a retailer near you, email info@cedarlanepress.com or visit us at www.cedarlanepress.com.

Index

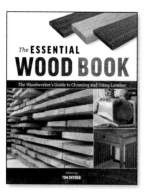
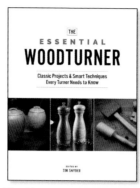

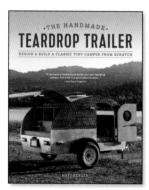
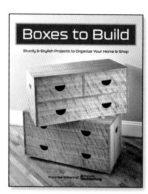
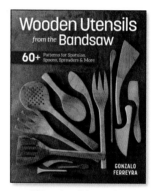